"Don't mistake the simplicity of this book for the punch it packs. Great leaders know how to love—a concept that has only been validated over two millennia and 40 consecutive years of profitability at Southwest Airlines. Barrett and Blanchard invite you into an extraordinary conversation between two extraordinary leaders. Don't miss it!"

—**Kevin & Jackie Freiberg**, coauthors of NUTS! *Southwest Airlines' Crazy Recipe for Business and Personal Success* and BOOM! *7 Choices for Blowing the Doors Off Business-as-Usual*

"*Lead with LUV* presents a lesson in the title itself. Being a fan of both Ken Blanchard and Colleen Barrett, I was delighted to listen in on this valuable conversation for creating high-performing leaders and teams."

—**Laurie Beth Jones**, author of *Jesus, CEO* and *The Path*

"Twenty-five years ago, when I became the training manager for *The Los Angeles Times*, the publisher asked me what my management philosophy was. 'The Gospel According to Ken Blanchard,' I replied. Today, as I read Ken's new book, *Lead with LUV*, I found myself smiling and nodding in agreement. Timeless wisdom is just that—timeless. It doesn't change with management fads. Through good times and bad, 'loving people to success' still delivers the highest dividends. And Southwest Airlines is living proof!"

—**BJ Gallagher**, coauthor of *A Peacock in the Land of Penguins: A Fable About Creativity and Courage*

"As a police chief and a leader in the social sector of our world, I believe servant leadership is essential to create and maintain an environment that results in productive leaders. It is obvious that if you follow the principles in this book, starting with a well-known value system and people with the right attitude who are treated the best, those people will pass that treatment along to your customers."

—**Larry Zacharias**, Chief of Police, University of Texas at Dallas; retired Chief, Richardson, TX Police Department

"I LUV this book! Two of the best-known and best-loved leaders of our generation share from both their heads and their hearts the lessons they have learned—in their businesses and in their lives—about how to lead with LUV."

—**Barbara A. Glanz**, speaker and coauthor of *The Simple Truths of Service*

"This is leadership at its best. You will love it."

—**Jim Blanchard**, retired Chairman and CEO, Synovus

Lead with LUV

Lead with LUV

A Different Way to Create Real Success

Ken Blanchard
Coauthor of *The One Minute Manager®*

Colleen Barrett
President Emeritus of Southwest Airlines

Vice President, Publisher: Tim Moore
Associate Publisher and Director of Marketing: Amy Neidlinger
Editorial Assistant: Pamela Boland
Operations Manager: Gina Kanouse
Senior Marketing Manager: Julie Phifer
Publicity Manager: Laura Czaja
Assistant Marketing Manager: Megan Colvin
Cover Designer: Chuti Prasertsith
Managing Editor: Kristy Hart
Senior Project Editor: Lori Lyons
Copy Editor: Gill Editorial Services
Proofreader: Kay Hoskin
Compositors: Gloria Schurick, Kim Scott
Manufacturing Buyer: Dan Uhrig

Pearson Education, Inc.
Publishing as FT Press
Upper Saddle River, New Jersey 07458

FT Press offers excellent discounts on this book when ordered in quantity for bulk purchases or special sales. For more information, please contact U.S. Corporate and Government Sales, 1-800-382-3419, corpsales@pearsontechgroup.com. For sales outside the U.S., please contact International Sales at international@pearson.com.

Printed in the United States of America

Fifth Printing February 2012

ISBN-10: 0-13-703974-3
ISBN-13: 978-0-13-703974-6

Pearson Education LTD.
Pearson Education Australia PTY, Limited.
Pearson Education Singapore, Pte. Ltd.
Pearson Education Asia, Ltd.
Pearson Education Canada, Ltd.
Pearson Educación de Mexico, S.A. de C.V.
Pearson Education—Japan
Pearson Education Malaysia, Pte. Ltd.

Library of Congress Cataloging-in-Publication Data

Blanchard, Kenneth H.

  Lead with LUV : a different way to create real success / Ken Blanchard, Colleen Barrett. -- 1st ed.
      p. cm.
  ISBN 978-0-13-703974-6 (hardback : alk. paper) 1. Leadership. 2. Communication in personnel management. 3. Job satisfaction. I. Barrett, Colleen. II. Title.
  HD57.7.B5583 2010
  658.4'092--dc22
                              2010024350

Ken would like to dedicate this book to his Mom, Dorothy Heidenreich Blanchard, who instilled leading with love in his heart at a very young age; and to his Dad, Admiral Ted Blanchard, who put these theories into action in his many leadership positions. This book is also dedicated to the Founding Associates and the dedicated people who have made The Ken Blanchard Companies a model of leading at a higher level.

Colleen dedicates this book to her personal family, most especially her dearly departed Mom, Barbara Hennessey Crotty Blanchard (although not blood related to Ken and Margie Blanchard, they were most definitely kindred spirits in matters of the heart); to her Southwest Airlines Family, most especially her mentor, Herb Kelleher; and to the many other wonderful folks with whom she has worked and played over the years due to their various connections to the two aforementioned families. She has been very blessed to have crossed their paths and she thanks them for teaching her how important love, support, hope, encouragement, fun, and warm embraces are to one's inner well-being and self-fulfillment.

Contents

Foreword

Ken Blanchard and Colleen Barrett are a philosophical match made in heaven.

I was overjoyed to be asked to write this foreword to their remarkable book because I passionately share their joint belief that the infusion of love is an essential, but oft overlooked, ingredient in any business organization that wants to be superlative for a long period of time, rather than just "successful" for a limited time.

Most people are looking not only for monetary security but also for psychic satisfaction in their work. That satisfaction is provided in our personal lives by the love and affection of family and friends. Why shouldn't a business simply be an enlargement of our circle of family and friends?

For more than forty years, in her relationships with the People of Southwest Airlines, Colleen Barrett has lived the leadership principles extolled by Ken Blanchard. She has ensured that no grief goes unattended; that no joy goes unshared; that each achievement is celebrated; and that those requiring help receive it.

She has made successes of People who thought they were destined for failure and has administered necessary discipline with care, thoughtfulness, understanding, and, ultimately, pure and unflinching justice leavened by mercy. And, always, her unadulterated focus has fastened on what is good, egalitarian, and right for ALL of the People of Southwest Airlines, not just a favored few.

For those who might think that leading with love is simply "soft management," review the record of Southwest Airlines over the last forty years. In a business so fraught with economic peril that the entire domestic airline industry has compiled a net loss since its inception, Southwest's People have produced an unprecedented and unparalleled record of job security, Customer satisfaction, and Shareholder return. From these results, it can factually and logically be concluded that if you seek long continued success for your business organization, treat your People as family and

LEAD WITH LOVE

Herb Kelleher
Founder and Chairman Emeritus
Southwest Airlines Co.

* * *

Once upon a time, there was a remarkable person who was known to lead with love.

Her company succeeded where almost all the other companies struggled with problems—from losing money to dealing with disgruntled customers to struggling with unhappy employees.

However, she and her team were remarkably successful. Employees loved to work there, customers were loyal, and the company was profitable year after year for decades.

This loving leader did not have a fancy business degree. In fact, she began her career as an executive secretary. Yet the founder of the company chose her to succeed him as president. When asked why, he said, "Because she knows how to love people to success."

Perhaps the most remarkable part of this story is that our heroine is a real person. Her name is Colleen Barrett, and she is President Emeritus of Southwest Airlines. Please enjoy getting to know her through the ongoing conversation that you are about to experience.

* * *

WHAT IS LEADERSHIP?

Ken: Colleen, it's a real honor to talk with someone who leads with love. Would you mind if I called you "The Love Manager"?

Colleen: Actually, Ken, I would mind, even if you spelled it LUV.

K: LUV?

C: LUV is our symbol on the New York Stock Exchange. We first started flying out of Love Field in Dallas, and our first advertising slogan in 1971 was "Southwest Airlines, the Someone Else Up There Who LUVs You." We also had a heart on our first signature line and letterhead. And today, forty years later, we still have hearts on our aircraft. So, frankly, if you have a need to put a label on what I do, I would prefer that you call me a LUVing Leader.

K: What do you have against the word manager?

C: Nothing, really. But as someone said years ago, "You can't manage a horse to water." So, at Southwest Airlines, although we have *Manager* titles, we prefer to use the word *Leader* because we want all our People to realize they have the potential to be a Leader; they can make a positive difference in anyone's work and life, regardless of whether they are in a management position. So we try to hire Leaders, no matter what role we want them to fill.

Talking about the roles People fill, in our internal Company communications, we highlight People's different roles by capitalizing their designation as well as their title. So anyone reading this conversation will notice that, when we refer to Southwest Airlines, not only are Pilot and Mechanic capitalized, but also words such as People, Employee, Leader, Customer, and Company. This is part of what our People call "Colleen's Bible."

K: I'm glad you said *part* of "Colleen's Bible," because I also know that some words that are normally two words or hyphenated words, such as *bottom line, team player,* or *check-in,* appear as one word in your "Bible." Because that might drive our non-Southwest readers crazy, we're not going to do that.

C: You mean I don't always get my own way?

K: No, because this is a coauthored work, and we don't want to send our editors into a tizzy.

C: Oh, all right. Geez Louise.

K: Colleen, I hope that everyone eavesdropping on our conversation will get the point you were making before we were interrupted with "Bible" talk: *Everyone has the potential to be a leader and have a positive influence on people they meet.* The reason I reiterate this point is that when I ask groups of managers around the country, "How many of you think you are a leader?" fewer than a third of them raise their hands.

C: Do you know why? Because somehow they think leadership is all about having a position or a title; therefore, leadership is something that is limited to only a few people—often top managers such as CEOs or presidents. I think Leadership is a way of life. All of us can be Leaders, both at work and in our homes and communities.

K: So we agree, then, leadership is an influence process.

Anytime You Seek To Influence The Thinking, Behavior, Or Development Of People In Their Personal Or Professional Lives, You Are Taking On The Role Of A Leader

C: That statement makes me happy, because if you continued to call me *The Love Manager*, we wouldn't have had a very good conversation. I consider myself a Leader, not a manager.

❤ **STOP AND THINK**

In the past, have you considered yourself a manager or a leader? If you have thought of yourself as a manager, how do you feel now, after sitting in on our conversation? If you accept our belief that you are a leader, who are you able to influence the most in your daily interactions at work, in your home, or in your community?

K: **When people have such strong feelings about leadership, I'm always interested in where those feelings came from. I love to ask people, "Who had the greatest impact on your life and who you are as a leader?" Hardly anyone ever mentions a manager or supervisor at work. They talk about their mother or father, a grandfather or uncle, or even their spouse or a friend.**

C: Bingo. When I think about who influenced my life the most as a Leader, I think of my Mother. She, more than anyone, taught me how to lead with love.

CELEBRATING SUCCESSES

K: Your Mother "done well!" I think your whole approach to leading and motivating People is about love. Don't you send out thousands of letters every year to your People, celebrating their successes and praising them for their efforts? That sounds pretty loving to me.

C: I guess it is, but I never did that all by myself. We have a small Internal Customer Care Team that, together with my personal staff, helps the Executive Office keep track of every Employee's birthday, Company anniversary, the birth of children, and other important events. This Team makes sure that cards go out for nearly every occasion. Our office sends out more than 100,000 cards annually. Many of our Officers hand-write several thousand notes each year. Besides being loving, we know this is meaningful to our People, because we hear from them if we miss something significant in their lives, like the high school graduation of one of their kids. We just believe in accentuating the positive and celebrating People's successes.

To sustain our Company Culture, we cheer People on all the time. We celebrate little things, big things—we celebrate everything! Although we do have some formal celebrations, a lot of them are informal, spontaneous celebrations that cost little or no money. For example, just giving People chocolates when something good has happened can make them feel like you've given them a million dollars. What's important is the fact that you're honoring them and acknowledging that what they do makes a positive difference. In the process, you are making heroes out of them. You are letting them know that you love them for their efforts and you want everybody to celebrate their success.

K: That's why I think you and I are soul mates, Colleen, because that's one of my core beliefs, too. If someone said to me, "Ken, from now on you can't teach anything you have taught or written about in the past except one thing; what do you want to hold onto?" I know exactly what it would be. I would want to continue to share the belief that the key to developing people and creating great organizations is to catch people doing things right and accentuate the positive by praising them.[1] It's all about celebrating a success that someone or a team has had. Celebrating successes has been a key part of my own leadership for a long time.

One other thing that's important about your philosophy, Colleen, is that you don't praise your People just for showing up; you celebrate specific things they have done. As Spencer Johnson and I emphasized in *The One Minute Manager*®, when it comes to One Minute Praisings, just wandering around and telling people, "Thanks for your effort," without being specific, has little meaning. But when you say to a woman who reports to you, "I just read your operational analysis report, and let me tell you, it was so clear. I loved the recommendations you made, particularly the cost-cutting suggestions. They will not only help us contain our costs, but also improve our efficiency"—that person will know you're sincere and really know what she is doing. The same approach works at home. "Alec, your mother showed me your report card. Three As and two Bs. Way to go! That's a real improvement from last semester."

C: We also try to make any cheering of People timely— as close to the event or performance as possible. I know that is another important element of a One Minute Praising.

K: It sure is. If a long time elapses between when someone does something right and when it is noticed, the praising loses its luster.

C: People hate waiting until their annual performance review to get all the good news or bad news.

❤ STOP AND THINK

Are you tired of all the praisings you get at work? At home? Do you wish people would lay off? Most folks laugh when they are asked those questions, because the reality is that catching people doing things right and celebrating their successes is not common practice at work, at home, or anywhere else. How are you doing with praising your people and celebrating their successes? When you get home at night, do you wander around and see what went *right* during the day? Try it with your people and your family, and they will be thrilled. And always remember to be immediate and specific.

K: Colleen, tell me: If you lead with love, how do you handle bad news—when someone is doing something wrong?

C: That's where another kind of love comes in. Some call it "tough love" because it may look like you are being tough. But I think sometimes the most loving thing you can do is to be straight with People when they are getting off course. Let me give you some examples:

- I had to let a personal staff member go because she did not display Golden Rule behavior with her peers. She played well "up" the ladder, so to speak, but not as well with folks she perceived to be at or below her position level. Her skills were top notch—it took two people to replace her—and it was very difficult for me. But it obviously had to be done.

- One of my best friends at work, who was also an exemplary Employee, had very little respect for her new boss and was becoming a different person from the one I had admired and loved. In a challenging conversation, I had to let her know that her supervisor would be staying in place for at least a couple of years and that if she couldn't find a way to recapture her once-positive attitude and make it work with him, she needed to leave.

- I've often had to tell good friends that I couldn't write them letters of recommendation or that I couldn't intercede regarding disciplinary action because my review of the facts didn't warrant those favors.

- Like most Leaders, I've been in a position over the years of having to support involuntary terminations due to circumstances. But in several cases I have been able to continue close personal relationships with these same folks after they left Southwest.

K: It sounds like you certainly don't let poor behavior or performance go unnoticed.

C: Absolutely not. And it's never easy or pleasant. But after dealing with it, if the person is still part of our Team, I watch him or her closely so that, as soon as possible, I can catch that person doing something right. I prefer praising and celebrating successes to dealing with problems.

❤ STOP AND THINK

How do you deal with inappropriate behavior or performance? Are you a seagull manager—do you fly in, make a lot of noise, dump on people, and then fly out? Or do you deal with people in a straight and loving way as soon as you observe inappropriate behavior? Is this an area where you need some work?

HAVING MENTORS

K: Where did your addiction to celebrating People's success and praising their efforts come from, Colleen?

C: Once again, I would have to say it was from my Mother. She had a huge heart. She not only loved and cared for people, she respected them. Although she didn't actually use the expression, she modeled The Golden Rule:

Do Unto Others
As You Would Have Them
Do Unto You

Mom's guiding belief in life was that if you are good to others, others will be good to you. As long as you were respectful of others and treated people the way you would like to be treated, you would get that back in kind.

As a result of my Mother's influence, my biggest expectation with our People is that they be egalitarian in nature. When I use the word *egalitarian*, I mean that everybody has the right to be treated with respect, and everyone should be required to treat others with respect. And, perhaps more importantly, everyone has an equal opportunity to contribute to the overall success and well-being of the Company.

Our mission at Southwest is "dedication to the highest quality of Customer Service delivered with a sense of warmth, friendliness, individual pride, and Company Spirit." But you don't have to know the mission word for word if you're an Employee—although most can probably quote it to you—as long as you know that the number-one expectation is that you will practice The Golden Rule every day in a loving way.

"Colleen teaches us that
love is what matters and that
you have to lead with your heart
and know that the heart
will take you in the right direction."

—Kevin Krone, VP Marketing, Sales, and Distribution

K: How did your Mother teach those values to you?

C: Using your terms, Ken, she constantly caught me doing things right. In fact, I have a great story about my cheerleading Mom.

A few years ago, I received a special airline industry award, the Tony Jannus Award. I was the first female to receive it, so I felt honored. But I don't like having attention called to myself; I just hate the limelight. At this formal gathering, there were some five hundred people in the audience, including all the honchos of the airline and aviation industries. Also in attendance were a few special friends like Kevin and Jackie Freiberg, who together wrote *Nuts,*[2] a wonderful book about the People of Southwest Airlines. I also invited my baby brother (my other brother had died many years earlier at the tender age of 21) and other relatives, a number of whom I hadn't seen in years. My family isn't very large anymore, so all of them were seated in the front at one table.

I'm not in the habit of making prepared remarks. But Herb Kelleher, the Founder of Southwest Airlines who had received this particular award years earlier, told me that for this event I had to have prepared remarks. It was that important. I fretted for a week. I really worked on these remarks and was finally satisfied. On the night of the awards ceremony, I didn't even dare have a glass of wine. I sat through the big presentation with this award hanging over my head. It felt like it weighed about five hundred pounds. Finally, after I was introduced, I went to the podium to make my remarks. Unbeknownst to me, my brother had snuck in twelve cowbells. As I was about to speak, my whole family stood up and rang those cowbells.

When that happened, my first response—besides getting really choked up—was to think: Oh my gosh, now all these people are going to realize that I am nothing but a hick from the sticks of Vermont! Then I just lost it. I got so choked up that I could not talk, nor could I see the words of my prepared remarks. So I skipped my prepared remarks and just talked from my heart, as I am prone to do. I was emotional as I explained that the rowdy group with the cowbells was my family. Then I told them the significance of the cowbells.

When I was growing up in Vermont, we didn't have much of anything, but we had a lot of love in our family. We lived on top of a hill in a little house. There was really no place to play, so we had to go across to a cemetery that was parallel to our road. When it was time for us to come in from playing in the cemetery, my Mother would ring an old cowbell.

Over the years, this foolish cowbell became like an announcement of anything that was important in our family. For example, if somebody got an A on their report card, Mom would ring the cowbell. Or if we had company coming, my Mother would go out and ring the silly cowbell. The people on the street never knew what was going on, but when they heard the cowbell, they knew something was going on at the Crotty (my maiden name) household! When our house burned down, that foolish cowbell was burned to the point that it didn't work. So Mom kept the old cowbell, got another one that worked, and the tradition went on. She did this until she died.

After that awards night, Herb said that my acceptance was the best speech I'd ever made. My values showed through.

K: I wish I had been there. It must have been a hoot. It sounds like Herb Kelleher has been an important role model for you, too.

C: He has, Ken. In the world of work, I couldn't have had a better teacher, coach, or mentor than Herb. At the beginning of my career when I first met Herb, he had been at his law firm for ten years and had never had a full-time secretary. He just sort of went around and passed out his work, and whoever was available typed it. He also had not opened a single file. That was when I knew that he really needed me. He literally had two offices at this law firm: one that he worked in, and another that had no furniture whatsoever—only files and stacks of paper all over the floor. You cannot imagine what a mess it was. So I thought, as his executive secretary, I would save him, and I guess you would say the rest is history.

Herb and I are so different. It truly is a miracle that we've survived forty-plus years of working together, but I think it's because we're so different. Herb is really brilliant and incredibly visionary. And back then, especially, he would see the vision but he wouldn't have any idea how many steps you had to take to get there; he would just want it done. At that time, I was pragmatic and systematic and quite organized. So that's how our team, or partnership, started.

For many years as Herb's executive secretary, I was so naïve and inexperienced that I don't think I appreciated what he was doing for me when he took me under his wing. All Herb ever really wanted to do was practice law. He didn't want to run an airline. It's just one of those things that evolved and happened. But he had a small group of five people (two lawyers, a law clerk, and me), and anything that he did, we did. I didn't know that that was unusual. If he went to Washington to lobby on something, I was there with him, as well as his law clerk. Whatever he did, we did. He always included us. We were all part of the team and part of the family. Herb was there to serve us, and we were there to serve him.

*"The first word that comes to mind is family.
You know—you treat your family the way
you want to be treated;
you care for them; you respect them.
And everywhere I go in my travels,
I see that in Southwest Airlines Employees."*

—Southwest Customer Eric Krueger

❤ STOP AND THINK

Take a minute to think about the people who have most influenced your thinking, behavior, and development as a leader. What did they do that impacted you, and where does that show up today in your various roles as a leader? Remember that sometimes negative influencers can be helpful, too. They model what *not* to do as a leader. Have you had any of those kinds of influencers in your life?

SERVANT LEADERSHIP IS LOVE IN ACTION

K: Colleen, talking about serving, I think you are a Servant Leader. Servant Leadership is love in action—and that's what you and Herb have been doing at Southwest for forty years.

C: I appreciate your calling me a Servant Leader, Ken, but when I mention that term to people, they often associate it with soft management. If I were to add that Servant Leadership is love in action, they would freak out! Love isn't a word that's used too often in corporate America. In fact, we've received some push-back about the very subject of this book.

❤ STOP AND THINK

What was your first reaction when you read "Servant Leadership is love in action?" Did you think about putting the book down, or were you excited to read on? Be honest!

K: You're right. Most people don't think love and leadership go together. Therefore, they want to know how we can lead with love. I think life constantly presents us with opportunities to choose love and serve one another, especially in our roles as leaders. Someone asked my wife, Margie, "You have been married to Ken for more than forty-five years. What do you think leadership is all about?" Margie nailed it. She said, "Leadership is not about love—it *is* love. It's loving your mission, it's loving your customers, it's loving your people, and it's loving yourself enough to get out of the way so other people can be magnificent."

C: Ken, you certainly married above yourself. I'm always blown away by Margie's wisdom. Indeed, we have tried to practice what she is saying throughout our history.

Most airline employees won't proudly confess in social settings that they're airline employees, because people always have an airline story, and it's usually a bad one. But we are really blessed. Nine times out of ten, if we say that we work at Southwest, people have a story about us, and it's a good one. The stories are filled with love and exemplify The Golden Rule in action. That makes me really proud. Let me tell you one of many memorable Southwest Airlines love stories.

A few years ago, we lost a much-loved Line Mechanic from Dallas, Roger Elliott, to cancer. Traditionally, Southwest has not shipped human remains, but we will do it for family members if there's a special need. So, because it was the right thing to do, we made plans to ship Roger's body from Dallas to his family in Detroit.

On the day Roger's body was going to be taken home from Love Field, we happened to be having a meeting in the downstairs training room at our headquarters in Dallas. One of the Mechanics in the room came over to me and said, "Colleen, Roger's plane is leaving in about ten minutes." He asked me if it was okay to leave the meeting for a few minutes to go out and stand at the fence.

Now, this was during the most brutal heat of the summer—hot enough that I usually don't go outside for ten minutes because I react poorly to heat. But I said, "Of course. We'll all go." So we did. There were over a hundred of us.

As luck would have it, there was a huge thunderstorm in Houston, where Roger's plane had to fly to on its way to Detroit. We pushed the plane back in Dallas and gave it a military-style salute, which was touching. Then the plane was put on a ground hold and it sat, and sat, and sat on the runway. It was so hot that one young woman actually fainted and was taken off by ambulance. Yet nobody went back inside. I mean, no one. I'll bet we stood out there for forty minutes. We actually missed an entire presentation in the meeting.

Some of the People standing at that fence didn't know Roger Elliott at all. In fact, some of them had never met the man. But he was one of our own, so when a few folks cried and started singing "Amazing Grace," everyone joined in. I received grateful notes from Roger's relatives who were on the airplane, watching us through the windows. They couldn't hear the words we were singing, but they understood right away what was happening, and it deeply touched them. They could feel our love.

UNDERSTANDING SERVANT LEADERSHIP

C: That's what Servant Leadership is all about. So it makes me sad when people hear the term *Servant Leadership* and, as you have said, they think you're talking about la-la land where the inmates are running the prison or trying to please everyone.

K: The problem is that they don't understand leadership or, more importantly, Servant Leadership. They think you can't lead and serve at the same time. Yet you can, if you understand that there are two kinds of leadership involved in Servant Leadership: strategic leadership and operational leadership.

Strategic leadership has to do with vision/direction. It's the *leadership* part of Servant Leadership. The focus for strategic leadership is the "what" that ensures everyone is going in the same direction. This is all important because:

Leadership Is About
Going Somewhere—
If You And Your People Don't Know
Where You Are Going,
Your Leadership Doesn't Matter

Alice learned this lesson in *Alice in Wonderland* when she was searching for a way out of Wonderland and came to a fork in the road. "Would you tell me, please, which way I ought to go from here?" she asked the Cheshire Cat. "That depends a good deal on where you want to get to," the cat said. Alice replied that she really did not much care. The smiling cat told her in no uncertain terms, "Then it doesn't matter which way you go."

C: We've always tried to make sure everyone knows where we are heading. Then, of course, we had to make it all happen.

K: In essence, that's what operational leadership is about: implementation—the "how" of the organization. This is the *servant* part of Servant Leadership. It's what leaders focus on after everyone is clear on where they are going. It includes policies, procedures, systems, and leader behaviors that cascade from senior management to frontline employees and make it possible for the organization to live according to its vision and values and accomplish short-term goals and initiatives. These management practices create the environment that employees and customers interact with and respond to on a daily basis.

C: As Julie Andrews sang in *The Sound of Music,* "Let's start at the very beginning—a very good place to start..." I'd love to hear what you think effective strategic leadership involves, Ken.

THE TRIPLE BOTTOM LINE

K: It's all about having the right target—the triple bottom line,[3] a compelling vision, and short-term goals and initiatives.

C: Slow down a minute, Ken. I have a sense of what the triple bottom line is, but what does it mean to you?

K: If you don't mind, I would love to hear your philosophy first, Colleen.

C: All right. Our entire philosophy of Leadership is quite simple: Treat your People right, and good things will happen. When we talk to our People, we proudly draw a pyramid on the chalkboard and tell them: You are at the top of the pyramid. You are the most important Person to us. You are our most important Customer in terms of priority. Therefore, I am going to spend 80 percent of my time treating you with Golden Rule behavior and trying to make sure that you have an enjoyable work environment where you feel good about what you do, about yourself, and about your position within this Company. But if I do that, what I want in exchange is for you to do the same thing by offering our Passengers—who are our second Customer in terms of priority—the same kind of warmth, caring, and fun spirit. If you do that consistently, our Passengers will recognize how significantly different this is from the behavior they witness at other businesses, and they will come back for more.

If they come back often enough and become loyal Customers, they will tell stories about us to their friends. Then we'll make money, which keeps your job secure and pleases our third Customer in terms of priority, which is our Shareholder—thus a win-win for all concerned.

❤ STOP AND THINK

Southwest puts their employees first, their customers second, and their shareholders third. How does your top management prioritize these three? It might not be as explicit as Southwest, but you know the ranking, don't you?

K: Colleen, you nailed it. A Servant Leader's energy is focused on not just the financial bottom line, but on three bottom lines: being the *employer of choice*, the *provider of choice*, and the *investment of choice*.

I recently read a wonderful thought from the Dalai Lama.[4] He said that companies are living, complex organisms—not profit-making machines. Therefore, profit shouldn't be the object of a company, but rather a result of good work. Just like a person can't survive for long without food and water, a company can't survive without profits—but no one would ever reduce the purpose and significance of human life to only eating and drinking.

Servant Leaders know that financial success is a byproduct of how their people and their customers are treated. I think we both believe, don't we, Colleen, that:

Profit Is the Applause You Get
For Creating A Motivating
Environment For Your People
And Taking Care
of Your Customers

C: I certainly do believe that, Ken. In fact, thanks for making the order of importance the Southwest Way. I think one of the problems with some leaders in business today is that they act like there's only one reason to be in business—to make money. They forget about their people and their customers.

K: I have a dream that someday there will be a list of "Fortunate 500" companies.[5] Right now, Fortune 500 companies are all about size and volume. For a company to be a "Fortunate 500" company, it would not only have to be profitable but would also need to have passionate, empowered people and loyal customers. If the company missed its numbers one quarter, the stock price might fall, but only a few points if its people and customers were loyal and loved the company. Companies that should be slammed on Wall Street are those that not only perform financially below projections but also those whose people are not engaged and whose customers are not loyal.

"I always wanted to work for Southwest Airlines.
When I started working in the airlines,
that's where I wanted to go.
I had to wait five years to get on with them
but it was well worth the wait."

—Tom McClane, Phoenix Aircraft Mechanic

Employer of Choice

C: I buy what you're saying, Ken. I think the goal of every company should be to be the employer of choice, the provider of choice, and the investment of choice. As you know, I think the entire success of a company begins with being the employer of choice. So let's start there.

K: Being the employer of choice today is challenging. With highly mobile, competent workers in demand, employers must find ways to attract and keep their best people. Good pay is no longer the only answer. It's true that some competent workers will go elsewhere for a higher wage; however, today's workers generally want more than pay. They seek opportunities where they feel that their contributions are valued and rewarded—where they are involved and empowered, can develop skills, can see advancement opportunities, and can believe they are making a difference.

C: We're so proud of our consistently low turnover rate. Combined voluntary and involuntary turnover has hovered around 5 percent for the past 25 years, and our voluntary turnover rate has always been 3 percent or less. This is truly incredible when you realize that turnover for the transportation industry as a whole has been in double digits for the last decade, with peaks ranging around the 20 percent mark.

We try in every way to let our Employees know they are important and are empowered to make a positive difference on a daily basis. That's one of the reasons why, in our corporate headquarters in Dallas, there is a huge inscription on the glass elevator wall in our lobby that says:

*The People of Southwest Airlines
are the creators of what we have
become—and of what we will be.
Our People transformed an idea
into a legend.
That legend will continue to grow
only so long as it is nourished—
by our People's indomitable Spirit,
boundless energy, immense goodwill,
and burning desire to excel.
Our thanks—and our love—to the
People of Southwest Airlines for
creating a marvelous Family and
a wondrous airline!*

K: I know how central that is to your way of thinking, Colleen. That's why I laughed out loud when I saw the sign on your office door that says:

I can only please one person per day.
Today is not your day.
Tomorrow doesn't look good either.

My wife Margie says I have an unusual sense of humor. I think you might have one, too!

C: We do think it's very important to always show a healthy sense of humor. We've told new hires the same thing for years—we want them to take our business seriously, but we don't want them to take themselves too seriously. I hope all of our People know how central they are to any success we've had.

We often say that other airlines can copy our business plan from top to bottom, but Southwest stands apart from the clones because of our People and how we treat them. But I would still wager that if another company somehow managed to hire all of our fantastic People, that company might see its best performance but still wouldn't match up to Southwest.

K: Why?

C: Because the new employer wouldn't possess the Southwest Culture—the secret sauce, if you will, of our organization. That Culture motivates and sustains us. So, for many of us, being part of our Company is not just a vocation—it's truly a mission. I don't dictate the Culture; none of our Officers do. Rather, it stems from the collective personality of our People. And they are what make us the provider of choice in the airline industry.

💚 STOP AND THINK

Where would you rate your organization or department on a one (low) to ten (high) scale on being the employer of choice? What can you do to improve your score?

Provider of Choice

K: It isn't easy to be the provider of choice in today's marketplace. Competition is fierce as new competitors emerge unexpectedly. Customers are more demanding because they have many more options at their fingertips. They expect to get what they want when they want it, and they want to have it customized to suit their needs. The world has changed in such a way that today the buyer, not the seller, is sitting in the driver's seat. These days, nobody has to convince anybody that the customer reigns. People are realizing that their organizations will go nowhere without the loyalty and commitment of their customers. Companies are motivated to change when they discover the new rule:

Today
If You Don't Take Great Care
Of Your Customers,
Somebody Else Will.

C: That's for sure! So great Customer Service has to be top of mind for all of your People. We emphasize that all the time. I love the way you and Sheldon Bowles challenged us all to create Raving Fans®, not simply satisfied customers.[6]

K: We think enthusiastic Raving Fan customers make your business a great business. Today you can't be content to simply satisfy customers. Raving Fan customers are customers who are so excited about the way you treat them that they want to brag about you—they become part of your sales force. Let me give you a simple yet powerful example of this, from an experience I had personally with your airline.

What usually happens when you call most airlines to either make or change a reservation? You get a recording that says, "All of our agents are busy right now, but your business is very important to us, so please stay on the line and we will be with you as soon as possible." Then the music starts. You could be on hold for who knows how long, sitting and waiting to talk to a human being. Recently, I called Southwest to change a reservation. Normally at Southwest, a human being picks up the phone. This time, a recording said, "I'm sorry, our Customer Service Agents are all busy right now; but at the beep, please leave your name and telephone number, and we will call you back within ten minutes." So that's what I did. What do you think happened a few minutes later? My cell phone rang, and this pleasant voice said,

"Is this Ken Blanchard?"

I said, "Yes."

"Ken, this is Bob from Southwest Airlines. How may I help you?"

Colleen, I've never had that experience with any other airline. How did you make that happen?

C: That's a feature that's available to all airlines. It's called *virtual queuing*. It helps us handle our heaviest calling times without lowering our Customer Service standard.

K: Why would Southwest use such a feature when no other airline seems to be doing it?

C: We're always looking for service capabilities that far exceed those of the competition, and that even exceed Customer expectations. Being called back by an airline? It was beyond most Customers' belief. Yet we routinely try to do the unexpected so we can then enjoy the growth and good reputation generated by Customers like you, Ken, who have spontaneously joined our sales force by bragging about us.

We recognize that the publicity we get from stories our Raving Fan Customers share about how our Employees treat them is more valuable and revenue-generating than advertising. Here are a few examples:

Our Flight Crews are always thinking of creative ways to make flights interesting and fun for our Passengers. I think a lot of them must have colored outside the lines when they were children.

> *Dear Southwest,*
>
> *I want to tell you about an experience I had recently that made me fall in love with you guys all over again. I was on Flight 3077 from San Diego to Denver when the flight attendant made an unusual announcement.*
>
> *"Okay, folks," he began, "I gotta be honest with you. It's been a really long day for us. To tell you the truth, we're tired."*
>
> *A few passengers giggled at that. These Southwest people were funny.*
>
> *"Ordinarily," the flight attendant continued, "this is the part of the flight when we announce that we'll be passing out peanuts and crackers for you all to snack on. But as I said, we're tired. So instead of passing them out, we're going to put them in a big pile up here at the front of the plane. When the plane takes off, the peanuts are going to slide down the center aisle. If you want some, grab 'em."*

There were a few more chuckles from the passengers—including me—as we fastened our seatbelts and prepared for take-off. I assumed he was joking.

I assumed wrong. The flight attendant dumped an ankle-high pile of packaged peanuts into the center aisle. Thanks to the law of gravity, when the plane took off at a steep angle, those peanuts began sliding toward the back of the plane.

What an icebreaker! Everybody started laughing. People in the aisle seats grabbed peanuts and passed them over to passengers who stretched out their hands.

"You thought I was kidding?" the flight attendant asked over the loudspeaker. "LOL," he deadpanned.

I only wish I could have videotaped the rest of that flight attendant's performance, because it was better than many of the shows I'd seen at comedy clubs. I reached Denver feeling happy and hopeful about the human race. That's a lot of value for one flight, which is why I remain a loyal Southwest fan.

—Customer M. Carroll Lawrence

We consider it a privilege to acknowledge the service of the brave men and women on active duty in our armed forces. It's the very least we can do.

Dear Sir/Madam,

I am writing to comment and gratefully acknowledge the fine service my husband and I recently received on one of your planes.

My husband returned to Norfolk, Virginia, after being deployed in Iraq for one year. Our flight home from Baltimore to Long Island was the last leg of a long journey for him. This flight became an unforgettable, beautiful memory for us both.

Your employee, a flight attendant named Sandra, took the time and effort to not only thank my husband for his service but asked that everyone on the plane do the same before exiting by allowing us to get off the plane first. As we began to exit, the passengers clapped, thanked, and congratulated us. We both began crying during Sandra's detailed announcement about my husband's service and our life together, and continued crying as we made our way up the aisle of the plane. It was such a relief to finally believe that someone appreciated the sacrifices we, and our children, had made.

As touched as we were by what went on inside the plane, we were floored to find that your employees on the ground were waiting outside the plane to present my husband with a bottle of champagne as well as their thanks. I was extremely touched when one of the Southwest employees turned to me to say, "Let me also thank you for what must have been a difficult year."

As we entered the gate area, every person waiting at the gate to depart stood and applauded the safe return of a man they had never met, based solely on the actions taken by Sandra.

Please extend our greatest appreciation for Sandra's creation of our treasured memory, which will last a lifetime.

—Customers Deborah and Peter Ellison

Going out of their way to help a Customer in need is all in a day's work for our People.

Dear Southwest,

> I am writing to relay my deep appreciation for the care exhibited by one of your flight attendant, Dina A. I am an extremely fearful flyer and try to avoid it whenever I can. On July 3, I needed to fly alone to Chicago for a family funeral. Dina was the reason I was able to make it! She helped me talk to the pilots before we took off, sat with me for parts of the flight, and was a warm, supportive, and reassuring presence throughout. She never made me feel silly or ashamed of my fear. She was like a dear friend who knew all the right things to say. I hope you will pass along my deep gratitude to Dina. I will be forever grateful for her kind patience.

> —Amy, a Raving Fan Customer

As a Mother, I can't imagine anything more important than knowing my child would receive tender loving care if he needed to fly alone.

Dear Southwest Airlines:

I'm writing to thank you for the excellent service Southwest has provided our family. Our 11-year-old son has traveled several times with you as an unaccompanied minor, and it is always uneventful. Recently he once again geared up for a flight to grandma's house. When the second leg of the flight was delayed, we got a call from him letting us know. It was a nice touch when the pilot came on the phone and let us know the exact situation and reason for delay. We were surprised the captain took the time to speak to us personally. We instructed our son to eat the snacks we had sent with him since dinner would be delayed, and not to get in the crew's hair while they were grounded.

Imagine our surprise when we later found out that the captain took our son to dinner with the rest of the pilots to the airport McDonald's. For an 11-year-old, hanging out with the pilots was really cool! The captain could have easily left someone to babysit our son while they got dinner, but by including him, it made his day.

Southwest has once again confirmed that it is a people-oriented, truly friendly operation. We will keep coming back.

—Customers Kristine and Glen Smith and son Nico

K: Wow! Those are great Raving Fan Customer Service stories. Keeping your customers happy is definitely one of the best ways to ensure that the cash is flowing.

❤ **STOP AND THINK**

Where would you rate your organization or department on a one (low) to ten (high) scale in terms of being the provider of choice? Do you have any great customer service stories that have become legendary around your organization?

Investment of Choice

K: That leads me to the third aspect of the triple bottom line—the investment of choice—which Southwest certainly has been for the past four decades. To me, the financial success of an organization is a function of revenue minus expenses. You can become more financially sound either by reducing costs or increasing revenues. Let's look at costs first, because in today's competitive environment, the prize goes to those who can do more with less.

C: Unfortunately, many organizations are deciding that the only way for them to manage costs and be financially effective today is to downsize. There's no doubt that some personnel reduction is necessary in large bureaucracies where everyone has to have an assistant, and the assistant has to have an assistant. Yet downsizing is an energy drain, and it's by no means the only way to manage costs. We started with a pared-down, efficient organization and have stayed that way, so downsizing has not been a big issue.

K: I applaud you for that, Colleen. You also do another thing very well: You treat your People as your business partners when it comes to managing costs.

Treating your People as your business partners is particularly important in uncertain times. I was blown away when I had the privilege of being at a meeting of all of Southwest's key Leaders during the spell of sky-high gas prices in 2008. Gary Kelly, your Chairman, President, and CEO, was open with everybody about how this was impacting the financial bottom line, and he solicited everyone's suggestions and help. It appears to me that, to your leadership, your People are your business partners. That philosophy certainly is not universal throughout corporate America. Why? Because most corporate leaders do not believe an important truth that the leadership at Southwest practices, which is:

*If You Keep Your People Well Informed
And Let Them Use Their Brains,
You'll Be Amazed At How
They Can Help Manage Costs*

C: I am proud of the cost-cutting savings that have come from treating our People as our business partners. Let me give you some examples.

One of our Flight Attendants suggested we take our logo off our trash bags, which had been color printed—this saved us about $100,000 a year. Our Flight Attendants also noticed how many fresh lemons were going to waste on every flight because very few Passengers asked for them, so we eliminated lemons and have saved a lot of money that way. One of our biggest cost savings occurred when some of our Employees, on their own, built the www.southwest.com website, which saved hundreds of thousands if not millions of dollars. And an extraordinary example of our People helping the Company was during Desert Storm, when the cost of fuel was very high. Our Employees came up with a program called Fuel from the Heart, whereby they could sign up to have a certain amount of money withdrawn from each paycheck to help the Company with the cost of fuel.

K: Great stuff, Colleen—particularly that last one. So the key is to first treat your People as your business partners. Then they will trust you and want to help the Company manage costs.

C: We've certainly found that to be true over the years.

❤ STOP AND THINK

In these tough economic times, how have you managed costs? Were your people treated as business partners in this area?

K: Let's switch gears now. If you listen to your People and make them your business partners when it comes to managing costs, I'll bet, if given the chance, they can help you with revenues, too.

C: They sure can. For example, Ken, I know you have been the beneficiary of a new Customer initiative called the Business Select Fare, which was an idea generated by Southwest Employees. This is focused on Customers who don't mind spending a little extra money so they can be among the first fifteen Customers to board, ahead of almost everybody else, along with a few other perks.

K: Like a free drink! I'll bet Business Select has brought in significant new revenue for you all.

C: You'd better believe it. That program has generated millions of dollars since we initiated it.

We think having our People help generate revenue ideas is so important, we formed a Grow Revenue Strategy Team in 2001 that carried on, in a more structured way, our tradition of listening to suggestions from Employees. This team consisted of individuals from several departments as well as our Executive Planning Committee. Over the years they implemented many revenue-generating ideas including our Early Bird fare, our Bags Fly Free program, our PAWS (Pets Are Welcome on Southwest) program, and our "cashless cabin" policy. Although the Grow Revenue Strategy Team doesn't exist as such today, various task forces and special temporary committees have evolved from that Team that still listen and react to Employee suggestions. Ideas generated by our People over the years have influenced many important decisions ultimately made by our Executive Planning Committee.

So our People really *are* our business partners when it comes to not only managing costs but also increasing revenues.

♥ **STOP AND THINK**

What revenue-generating ideas have come from your people in these tough times? Do you even think that is their role? Where would you rate your organization or department on a one (low) to ten (high) scale for being the investment of choice in terms of managing costs and increasing revenue?

K: I think your Bags Fly Free advertising campaign was a stitch. And that policy has generated even more Raving Fan Customers. I hear people bragging about not having to pay extra for baggage on your flights.

Southwest certainly covers all the bases of the triple bottom line: employer of choice, provider of choice, and investment of choice.

❤ STOP AND THINK

Of the three aspects of the triple bottom line, which is your greatest strength and where do you need the most improvement in your department or organization? Do you sometimes overemphasize the financial side to the detriment of your people and your customers?

MAKING UNIONS YOUR BUSINESS PARTNERS

K: Colleen, I think what drives your success with the triple bottom line is your unwavering desire to treat your People as your business partners in every way.

C: There is no doubt about that in my mind. Without our People, we would never be able to create Raving Fan Customers or be sound financially.

K: Talking about treating your People like business partners, Colleen, a lot of folks don't realize that more than 80 percent of the People in your workforce are in unions. Most companies with unions wouldn't look at those People as their business partners but rather as adversaries.

C: That's the genius of Herb. When the first group of Employees had an opportunity to vote on whether they wanted to be part of a union, Herb told them, "I think unions are great, as long as we still sit on the same side of the table. I don't want, and I don't think you would want, a union whose leaders want to sit on the other side of the table." So our union folks participate in everything we do; their Leaders are involved in all major decision making. As business partners, we are on the same side of the table.

K: That's fabulous, Colleen. It's sad that there's so much win/lose in union and management relations in this country, not only in business but also in education.

❤ **STOP AND THINK**

If you have any unions in your organization, what are the union/management relations? If hostile, how can those relationships be improved? Getting people on the same side of the table is really important.

CITIZEN OF CHOICE

K: Colleen, I've often thought we should add a fourth aspect to this triple bottom line—citizen of choice. This is all about social responsibility. I'll bet you all do well there, too.

C: I think we do. We are not only concerned about our People, our Customers, and our financial well-being, but also about how we give back to the community. We have always encouraged our People to be active in their communities. We want them each to be the citizen of choice.

Working at our Company is what our Employees do, but it's not who they are. They are altruistic People with huge hearts and a deep passion for making a positive difference where they live and work.

To celebrate the countless acts of kindness demonstrated by our People, the Volunteers of LUV Award was created. Following are a few of 2009's award recipients: **Jennifer Jauregui-Burklow**, Burbank Operations Agent, who works with the USO helping soldiers who are both leaving for and returning from deployment; **Christal Campbell**, Phoenix Center Support Leader, who spent a week's vacation as a camp counselor at Camp Courage, a camp for young burn survivors; **Kevin Golding**, Nashville Operations Agent, who is a Big Brother to a twelve-year-old fatherless boy; **Jadira Simmons**, Phoenix Provisioning Agent, who coordinated a drive to supply 200 filled school backpacks to children in need; **Coetta Smith**, San Antonio Center Customer Rep, who prepares and delivers meals to senior citizens every week; and **Pat Rodriguez**, Technology Sr. Analyst, who works with three different animal welfare agencies to find adoptive homes for stray pets.

This is a small example of how our Employees are just as committed to community service as they are to Customer Service.

❤ STOP AND THINK

Is community service and being a citizen of choice important to you and your organization? How would a focus on this help improve the performance of your organization?

A COMPELLING VISION

K: Maybe we ought to add citizen of choice to our criteria for being a "Fortunate 500" company.

C: Good idea, Ken. Let me circle back to another aspect about having the right target or vision/direction that you mentioned: a compelling vision. I think I know what you mean by that, but tell me more.

K: This is a really important concept that many companies miss. To me, having some clarity about a compelling vision is crucial. Two of my colleagues— Jesse Stoner, who has been studying the impact of vision on organizational effectiveness for almost three decades, and Drea Zigarmi, our Director of Research and Development—identified three key elements of a compelling vision[7]—one that would inspire people and provide direction:

- *Significant purpose*—What business are you in?

- *A picture of the future*—What will the future look like if you are successful?

- *Clear values*—What guides your behavior and decisions on a daily basis?

To us:

*A Compelling Vision Tells You
Who You Are
(Your Purpose),
Where You Are Going
(Your Picture of the Future),
And What Will Guide Your Journey
(Your Values)*

A Significant Purpose

K: Without a significant purpose, leaders in organizations focus on their own agenda and personal enrichment. Employee loyalty and passion often go out the window as the point of work becomes simply to get as much as you can for as little effort as possible.[8]

C: I think a higher purpose is something that takes precedence over any short-term goal like profit.

K: It sure does. A significant purpose is your organization's *real* reason for existence. It answers the question "Why?" rather than just explaining what you do. It's what permits you to have a *both/ and* philosophy toward people and results. When that happens, the development of people—both employees and customers—is of equal importance to performance. In other words, it clarifies, from the viewpoint of your people and your customers, what business you are *really* in and where they fit into the equation.

Most companies either don't have a purpose statement or the one they have is way too complicated. A while back, I worked with a large bank. When I got in front of all the key managers, I said, "I certainly appreciate your sending me your purpose statement. Ever since I got it, I have slept much better. I put it next to my bed in case I woke up in the middle of the night. If that happened, I would just read your purpose statement and it would put me right back to sleep."

They all laughed because their purpose/mission statement rambled on and on. I felt it couldn't motivate a flea.

I told them if I were a customer of their bank, I would hope they were in the *peace of mind* business. If I gave them money, I would like to have the peace of mind that they would take care of my money and even grow it. I asked them whether they would rather be in the financial services business or in the peace of mind business. The advantage of being in the peace of mind business is that everybody—both employees and customers—understands what that means. For example, if a teller is rude to a customer, how is that helping that customer's peace of mind?

Colleen, what is the significant purpose at Southwest? What business are you in?

C: We're in the Customer Service business—we just happen to provide airline transportation. It's that simple. But it focuses all the energy of our People on taking care of our Customers. We have never purported to be all things for all people. We have always been very clear that if people will agree to purchase our services, we will attempt to give them an exemplary return on their investment. That is, we will do our best to assure they have a safe, on-time flight, for a reasonable price, with as little stress as possible, in a caring environment.

❤ **STOP AND THINK**

What business is your company or department in? Does everyone know it?

A Picture of the Future

K: The second element of a compelling vision is having a picture of the future. This picture of the end result should not be abstract. It should be a mental image you can actually see. For instance, at Disney theme parks, since they are in the happiness business, their picture of the future is that all guests should have a bigger smile on their face leaving the park than they had when they entered three, six, nine, or twelve hours before.

Colleen, what's the picture of the future at Southwest?

C: Our picture of the future is that every American has the "Freedom to Fly"—to be with friends, business associates, or relatives on happy occasions as well as sad ones. To make that happen, we want to keep our costs low (resulting in low fares) while maintaining an efficient, reliable way to fly. We also want people to enjoy flying, so we want to keep our spirits high (warm, friendly, and fun-spirited Employees), which all amounts to Legendary Customer Service.

When we were just starting out, we wanted to "democratize the skies." To understand that statement, you have to realize that back in 1971 when we put our first plane in the air, generally speaking, only rich people flew for pleasure. There were few women in business, so flying was done mostly by businessmen traveling on expense accounts. Our vision was that we would turn the status quo totally upside-down so that all people would be able to afford to fly for both business and pleasure. We wanted to convince the public that flying was not just for the elite.

K: In many ways, that's similar to the vision Bill Gates originally had for the computer industry. He wanted a computer on every desk and in every home, not just a select few.

C: I never thought about that, Ken. I guess Bill Gates wanted to democratize the computer industry!

❤ STOP AND THINK

Does everyone in your organization or department know what will happen if you do a great job living your purpose? How clear is your picture of the future?

"It started with Herb and Colleen...
and Gary Kelly now—they care for their Employees.
They genuinely care for us.
And so we think it's our duty to care for others, too.
That's why we like our Customers and we like to give
back. So as long as we have that Culture, I think that's
what makes us unique."

—Alex Ponzio, Dallas Captain

One final point regarding our delivery of Customer Service is a simple fact that most organizations do not seem to understand: There should be no difference whatsoever between your principles and values when delivering internal Customer Service versus external Customer Service. The Golden Rule applies there too, for goodness' sake!

K: You are so right. Some of the worst customer service can occur internally—within an organization itself. In many companies, if you call another department you think you're talking to an adversary. This can happen not only at work, but also at home. The sad reality is that most people treat folks they work with or love worse than they treat customers or total strangers. Suppose you had a party at your house and new neighbors came. Just after they leave, you notice that the man left his hat and you run out into street to hail him down. When you hand him his hat, would you say, "You idiot! If your head weren't screwed on, it would fall off!" Of course not. You'd say, "I'm glad I caught you. Here's your hat. Great to see you." And yet, we hear mothers shouting awful things at their kids when they've left their lunch behind. So yes, Colleen, internal customer service should be Legendary Service, too.

❤ STOP AND THINK

This is an important point. How is your internal customer service? Does it compare to your external customer service?

Clear Values

C: I guess it comes down to your values.

K: You got it. In fact, that's the third and final element of a compelling vision: having clear, guiding values. I know this is another one of your strengths at Southwest. Why? Because high-performing organizations have values they actually live by— something most organizations don't have.

Most organizations that do have values have too many—eight, ten, or twelve. They're for God, mother, and country, and everything else in between. In this case, more is not better. We have found that people can't focus on more than three or four values, if those values are to guide their behavior.[9] We also found that organizations must prioritize values for them to be effective. Why? Because life is about value conflicts. When these conflicts arise, people need to know which value they should focus on.

C: We're on the same page there, Ken. The highest priority for all of our Employees is safety, which we never compromise. Beyond that, we have identified three key values: Warrior Spirit, Servant's Heart, and Fun-LUVing Attitude.

K: Warrior Spirit sounds like you want fighters and battlers!

C: That's not what we mean by Warrior Spirit. Basically, it means that you have to have a fighting spirit to be successful. You want to be the best, work hard, be courageous, display a sense of urgency, persevere, and innovate. You want to be a winner. People don't want to work for a loser. You want to win at what you set out to do.

K: So it's a strong competitive spirit, but not in a warlike way.

C: That's right. It's similar to one of the two character traits that Jim Collins, in his book *Good to Great*,[10] used to describe great leaders: will, or resolve. It's the determination to follow through on a vision, mission, or goal. The focus is on giving your all to get the best result so everyone wins—your People, your Customers, your owners, and the communities in which you serve. We think there's nothing wrong with wanting to be the best at what you do.

"If you're willing to give 100 percent, this Company will always give you 100 percent back."

—Don Digregorio, Houston Ramp Supervisor

K: I would venture a guess that's what has made Southwest successful for almost four decades: Your people are true Warriors. They work hard and play hard. They work and fight to win.

C: We think that if in the beginning we had just been left alone by those big guys out there—the other airlines—we probably would have been out of business in two years. But we knew we had to fight to succeed and win.

Another reason we need People with Warrior Spirit is because we hire leanly—we don't want to furlough People. As a result, when we hire People, we're hoping to have them for life. Although we work lean at every level, due to our Warrior Spirit we have always been extremely productive.

The way we turn a plane is an example of our Warrior Spirit. With the understanding that safety is paramount, we work constantly to improve efficiency. You see, we make money when planes are in the air. So we went to our Dispatchers and Operational People and said, "We have to turn these airplanes in ten to fifteen minutes." And they said, "It's impossible." And we said, "It's not. You just have to have the mindset to do it."

Today, though we no longer have ten-minute turns, we still turn our planes faster than the other guys by far. Our vision in turning around a flight is to make it look like an Indianapolis 500 pit stop. When you pull into a gate and you're looking out the window, you will see our People gathered around, perched and ready to help turn that flight. If you fly on another airline, even when you go into their hub, you don't see that occur. It's fascinating to watch, and it's a mindset. There's a real team Warrior Spirit there. Everybody knows that everyone has an important role in that turnaround.

"I think it's easy when the weather is good,
the airplane's running on time—
anybody can look good in that environment.
It's when the weather goes bad,
we've had a mechanical (failure),
we've had a security breach—those types of issues.
That's when you really tell the mettle of an airline."

—Rod Jones, Phoenix Captain

K: Tell me about your second value: a Servant's Heart. To me, that's the core of knowing how to lead with love.

C: Absolutely. When we interview, hire, and promote, we're looking for People who are Servant Leaders—no matter what title or position they are going to hold, they have to want to serve. They need to have a Servant's Heart—a passion for serving others. We want all of our Employees to follow The Golden Rule, adhere to our basic principles, treat others with respect, put others first, be egalitarian, demonstrate Proactive Customer Service, and embrace the Southwest Airlines family.

I just love the kinds of things that result from this philosophy. I get calls from Passengers all the time who say things like, "I haven't seen Carroll Herzog (who is a Customer Service Agent for us in Houston) at Gate 41 for a couple of weeks; is something wrong?" Most companies don't have that happen. And we see it often. Or Carroll Herzog, the Customer Service Agent, will call and be in tears because she just read that one of her favorite Customers had a heart attack, is retiring, or whatever, and she wants to do something special for him or her.

"Colleen always says,
'Follow The Golden Rule,
learn from your mistakes,
and listen to your heart.'"

—Tammy Romo, Senior Vice President Planning

Our Passengers may not know all our names, but they know our faces, and they're not just conducting a business transaction with us—it's more personal than that. And that's what pays off. It's tangible in the sense that you can see it, but it's hard to quantify. But I know in my heart that it's huge. And I know in my heart that most companies are not lucky enough to have that kind of daily experience. Why? Because our People enjoy what they do, and they pass that joy onto our Customers.

I can't tell you how many letters we have received over the years from senior leaders of other companies who say, "I've tried to find the flaw; I've asked your people why they enjoy working at Southwest or to tell me what they don't like, and they'll always go back to the way you treat them and respect them and the way they trust your word and trust you." These letters always say, "I wish my people would talk about me that way."

K: Why do you get that reaction?

C: Because our People know that they can expect us to always treat them with respect. They know we think they are our most important resource. In contrast to the often repeated phrase, "The customer is always right," we recognize that there are times when the Customer is not right.

When Herb first made that statement many years ago and it appeared in a well-known publication, we received literally thousands of letters from people who thought it was a terrible statement to make for a Customer-oriented Company like ours. To flesh out this thought a bit, let me explain. We will not tolerate an Employee's physical or verbal abuse by a Customer, and we will back the Employee completely if we see this happening. I think it's important for our People to know we're on their side. At the same time, if our investigation shows that we were in the wrong, we will offer our profound apologies and make amends for our wrongdoings.

All of our Leaders try to model Servant Leadership. Herb led the way, clearly, although I don't think he even knew what the expression Servant Leadership meant until we told him. And to be honest with you, neither did I, until my friend Ann McGee-Cooper introduced me to the book *Robert K. Greenleaf: A Life of Servant Leadership* by Don Frick.[11]

But, while our recognition of the term *Servant Leadership* might have come late, for almost four decades Herb and I have said that our purpose in life as Senior Leaders with Southwest Airlines is to support our People. To me, that's what Servant Leadership is all about.

K: Colleen, with your emphasis on Customer Service and The Golden Rule, I'll bet you tell your People, "Don't ever ask anyone to do something that you wouldn't be willing to do right along with them."

C: That's an important part of The Golden Rule. It doesn't mean you can sit down on every project and work with them, but it does mean you're not above doing just that.

One of the most influential things that ever happened to me illustrates this. It occurred when I was a young secretary working with Herb. We had a mailer that had to get out, and everything that could go wrong with it went wrong. It had to be in the mail the next day. Well, the day before, the copy machine broke down and the postage was somehow wrong. So, all of these envelopes that had been stuffed had to be retyped, and this was not when you could just push a button and it would happen. You did it all yourself, manually. So it was about eight o'clock at night, the night they had to be postmarked, and we had to start all over again.

Herb sat right there with me until four o'clock in the morning, on the floor, licking envelopes and putting stamps on envelopes, because we didn't have a postage machine. I'll never forget it. My gosh. And he could have even thought that it was my fault that the mailing had gone wrong. But he didn't. He just jumped right in there with me. That was a really valuable lesson for me, so I've always tried to remember it and emulate it.

"We're all in it together.
No one's job is too important that they
can't pick up trash on the airplane.
The Pilots come back and help us
pick up trash during our quick turns.
Everyone's pitching in and helping each other."

—Candace Boyd, Dallas Flight Attendant

Just like Herb modeled for me, we want all decisions to be made from a Servant's Heart. When a person joins our Company, if we outline for them what our mission, values, and expectations are, in my mind they're making a pact and they're agreeing that they're going to follow that way of life. If they decide not to do this, we have two choices. The first is to give them a loving reprimand for not living up to our expectations. That's tough love. If that works, they are forgiven and they are back on the Team. If it doesn't, our second choice kicks in: career planning. We let them pursue their career someplace else. This doesn't mean they're bad people. It simply means that they no longer want to go where we are leading them and be a part of Southwest Airlines.

K: Garry Ridge, President of WD-40 Company,[12] has a wonderful way of describing this process:

When People Don't Fit
Your Company's Culture,
"Share Them With The Competition."

C: That's the ultimate in tough love, but I agree with that approach. If you let someone remain in your Company who doesn't buy into the Culture, it will create problems.

K: That's for sure. One of the important things I've learned over the years is that behavior is controlled by its consequences. If people thumb their nose at something you think is important, like your culture, and they don't get treated any differently than your best citizens, after a while people will begin to think that all the things you have been saying are important are just words—lip service.

❤ STOP AND THINK

Are people who don't live your values tolerated in your organization? If so, what has been the impact? If not, how are they dealt with?

C: That's one of the things I really like about Garry Ridge. He's not afraid to take a strong stand to protect his company's culture. He's also a fun-loving Aussie. That leads me to our third value, which is a *Fun-LUVing Attitude.*

K: That's another unusual value for corporate America.

C: I can't tell you how hard we worked on the proper descriptive we wanted to use. We ended up with "Fun-LUVing" to highlight our LUV symbol on the New York Stock Exchange.

Basically, a Fun-LUVing Attitude means just that: We want to *enjoy* our work life as much as we do our home life. We want to show each other and our valued Customers that we care about them, and we want them to feel like extended family members while they are in our presence. We have fun, we don't take ourselves too seriously, we maintain perspective, we celebrate successes, we enjoy work, and we are passionate Team players.

Now, we've been laughed at, we've been scoffed at, and we've been ridiculed for all of that; but I'll tell you, it works. You have to know your audience, and you have to be respectful of others. But having fun is part of our Culture. Our People are truly known for their sense of humor. The only time we've ever had a problem with that was right after 9/11, because it was such a tragedy for the whole nation, and humor wasn't appropriate then. So we toned things down for a while.

K: How do you find People with a good sense of humor?

C: We actually test for a sense of humor when we hire People. That's part of our application process. The first time Herb told our VP of People, which is our human resources area, that we wanted her to test for a sense of humor, she said, "Well, how the heck am I gonna do that? Should I put a whoopee cushion in their seat and see if they laugh?"

Actually, it's really easy to see if People have a sense of humor. It just takes your eyes and ears and observation. When we do group interviews as part of the hiring process, we might ask the group a question such as "How did you use humor to extricate yourself from an embarrassing situation?" Not only do we listen carefully to each applicant's response, we also like to watch the faces of the candidates who are *not* speaking and observe how they react to the interviewee's answer.

When we tell new recruits about Southwest during the orientation process, we give them a lot of history. We give them our legacy. We are great storytellers. Herb is probably the best storyteller I've ever met. I'm not as good as he is, but I learn every time he tells us stories. He has taught us to laugh at ourselves—to not take ourselves too seriously. We take our business seriously, but not ourselves, and we want our People to be that way, too.

> *"When I first started with the Company,*
> *everyone said, 'Hey, have fun, have fun.'*
> *The People who interviewed me—everybody—*
> *would say, 'Have fun. Be yourself. Have fun.'*
> *And so, when I got on board, I just started having fun.*
> *I just have a smile on my face, and it seems to rub*
> *off on people."*
>
> —Olander Coleman, Oakland Customer Service Agent

K: Your Fun-LUVing Attitude comes across every day to your Customers. I just laughed out loud one time when, after landing, I heard one of your Flight Attendants get on the microphone and say, "As we are taxiing, please keep your seat belts on. If you do stand up, we are going to send Bruno, our bag crusher, to the baggage claim area, and you're not going to like the condition of your bag."

I also love to hear the story that my friend, the great management author and speaker Patrick Lencioni, tells about your Fun-LUVing Attitude:[13] "You know something is a core value for a company if the people take it too far and create a problem, but the leaders are okay with it." He goes on to relate that someone wrote to Southwest and said, "I'm a long-time customer, and I don't like the fact that you make jokes during the safety announcement part of the flight."

Now, most companies would write back and say something like, "We value you as a customer. Please trust that we care about your safety. Here's a free flight coupon, and we'll talk to the flight attendants and correct the problem." And then they would send out an e-mail to tell their people that the humor and fun thing is good, but they need to tone it down.

When Patrick tells the story, at this point he always gets a big smile on his face when he says, "But not Southwest. No. They sent the customer a note that said, 'We will miss you.' That's when you know it's a core value—'We will miss you.'"

C: I love to hear Pat tell that story too, although it's not entirely true. The Customer he was talking about was not only complaining about our behavior during safety announcements, but about everything. This person wasn't a happy camper. That's what motivated us to say, "We'll miss you."

K: That's interesting. Once you become legendary in your service, your Customers and fans often exaggerate or even fabricate stories. I've never forgotten a great Nordstrom story. As you know, this great retailer has a reputation of taking anything back from a customer and reimbursing them with no questions asked. A popular story was that a customer brought back a pair of snow tires, and Nordstrom took them back even though they don't sell tires. That story became legendary, and in talking to Jim Nordstrom, one of the founders, years later, he laughed about that story. He said for a time they actually did sell snow tires in one store in Alaska, and that was where the customer returned the tires. That little detail was left out of the story by customers who spread it all over the country.

C: Whether Pat's story was exactly true or not, it does highlight how central fun is to our corporate culture. For example, I'll never forget when Tonda Montague, one of the original members of our Corporate Culture Committee, said to me, "I learned in the first few months of employment here not to schedule my vacation without checking the calendar, because there are certain days you don't want to miss being here—it's just too much fun." One of the days she was talking about was Halloween. We dress up in crazy outfits and have a lot of fun.

K: So you folks are real party animals!

C: Yes! But fun doesn't always have to mean parties with all the trimmings—although we do have a few of those every year—we call them Spirit Parties. Fun means we enjoy and celebrate life and each other in a laid-back, down-to-earth environment that is welcoming, warm, and enjoyable. It means we celebrate everything—both small and big victories and successes. It means we make a big deal out of the folks who "Live the Southwest Way," which means they display a Warrior Spirit, a Servant's Heart, and a Fun-LUVing Attitude on a daily basis. Sometimes we do this through special recognition events; sometimes with informal, spontaneous recognition ceremonies; sometimes with written celebratory congratulations in our newsletters; and sometimes with more formal awards. Our Annual Awards Banquet could give the annual Academy Awards ceremony a good run for its money!

We have picnics and barbeques and tailgate parties. We hold fundraising events for Employees down on their luck. We have all kinds of contests. We give showers for weddings and first births, and we throw retirement parties. We compete in many activities in which we give silly awards. We sponsor bowlathons, golf tournaments, baseball and softball tournaments, and ski trips. We have perfect attendance celebrations, and we give Winning Spirit Awards. We have a gazillion Employee recognition programs.

K: Why is a Fun-LUVing Attitude such a high value for you all, and worth sustaining?

C: Early in our history we occasionally flew on "the other guys," and we saw that there were no smiles, no warmth, and no enjoyment. It was all very robotic. Well, Herb can't be robotic, so we decided that we were going to have *fun* be an extremely important word at our Company. I think a number of companies try to do that today, but back then nobody was doing it. We decided *fun* was going to be a word we used a lot.

We made a decision that we didn't have to be stodgy or stuffy to be a successful business. It sounds kind of funny today, maybe, but when we first started talking to new hires, we didn't even want to use the word *professional*. Why? Because in the 1970s we thought that word denoted a "stiffness" that we didn't want. We wanted some light irreverence. We wanted some spirited fun. And—I hesitate to say the next thing just because of the generally uptight demeanor in today's social environment—we also wanted to be sexy. We thought the airline business could be, and should be, sexy. Now, I don't want to go down this trail too far, but the truth of the matter is that that was what Texas was all about at that time. So we did have girls wearing hot pants and go-go boots, and our first ad for Flight Attendants had the heading "We're looking for Raquel Welch lookalikes." What we were doing, of course, was getting the personalities that we needed and wanted for 1971, when the only people who were flying were Texas businessmen. Women weren't flying. So we knew our audience, and we went after them.

We stayed in those outfits about five years too long. I got the distinct pleasure of going in, with the head of our Flight Attendant union at the time, to tell Herb we were not going to wear those clothes anymore! That was a fun experience in and of itself. Herb knew we were right, but he never wanted to drop the fun from our way of doing business. What convinced him was his empathy: We told him the uniforms, selected by a prior CEO, were an embarrassment to wear in the early 1980s. So from that point on, our fun became more focused on our People and how they treated our Customers, rather than on what our People were wearing.

K: Colleen, it sounds to me like your culture, driven by your guiding values—a Warrior Spirit, a Servant's Heart, and a Fun-LUVing Attitude—permeates every aspect of your Company.

C: It is our essence, our DNA, our past, our present, and our future. Although these values are not officially rank-ordered, probably in practice they actually are. As I mentioned, safety is first. Then our next priority is getting the job done, and done well, for our Customers. That is driven by our Warrior Spirit. Yet we don't want to give our all without a Servant's Heart, expressed with a Fun-LUVing Attitude.

> *"In my view, when a brand understands that mission, core values, and stakeholder engagement (especially employees) are the essence of the brand, then that brand becomes sustainable.*
> *Southwest Airlines sets the standard."*
>
> —Rex Whisman, *Brand Champions* Blog

K: You all really nail the triple bottom line—or maybe I should say the quadruple bottom line—and have a compelling vision that is communicated throughout the organization. Strategic leadership is rounded out with short-term goals and initiatives that tell your People what you want them to focus on right now. But now those things take on more meaning because they are tied to a bigger picture.

C: Sure, we have annual goals and initiatives that we want our People to focus on. But the big picture is what we want them also to focus on all the time—our compelling vision and the quadruple bottom line.

♥ STOP AND THINK

Do you have a few well-established values for your organization or department that guide everyone's behavior? If not, that would be important to establish once everyone knows what business you are in (your purpose) and where you are going (your picture of the future). Name a leader in any industry and they each have a compelling vision: Disney in entertainment, Nordstrom in retail, Chick-fil-A in quick-service restaurants, Ritz-Carlton in hospitality, Wegman's in the grocery business, WD-40 in the "squeak and clean" business, Synovus in financial services and, of course, Southwest Airlines in the airline business.

WHAT MAKES SERVANT LEADERSHIP WORK?

K: Amen! Now let's see if we can put this all together. As we said, vision and direction are the *leadership* part of Servant Leadership. In establishing where you are going, the traditional pyramidal hierarchy is alive and well. That doesn't mean that top managers—I mean leaders—don't involve others in crafting this direction, but the responsibility for vision and direction falls to the hierarchical leadership. Kids look to their parents, players look to their coaches, and people look to their organizational leaders for direction. Max De Pree, legendary former chairman of Herman Miller and author of *Leadership Is an Art*, compared this strategic role to that of a third-grade teacher who keeps repeating the basics: "When it comes to vision, values, and direction, you have to say it over and over and over again until people get it right, right, right!"[14]

In a traditional organization, for the operational, or *servant*, aspect of Servant Leadership, hierarchical leaders are once again thought of as having sole responsibility, and people throughout the organization are taught to be responsive to their boss. "Boss watching" becomes a popular sport, and people are promoted based on their upward-influencing skills. That activity doesn't do much for accomplishing the strategic vision/direction. All people try to do is protect themselves, rather than move the organization in the desired direction.

Servant Leaders, on the other hand, feel their role is to help people achieve their goals. To do that, the traditional pyramid hierarchy is theoretically turned upside down so that the frontline people, who are closest to the customers, are at the top. Now *they* are responsible—able to respond—to the needs of the customers. In this scenario, leaders serve and are responsive to people's needs, training and developing them to soar like eagles so they can accomplish established goals and live according to the vision and values.

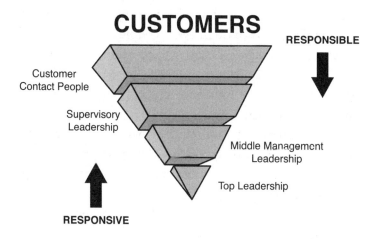

The Servant Aspect of Servant Leadership

C: When it comes to the servant aspect of Servant Leadership, Herb was my role model. He had no trouble philosophically inverting the traditional pyramidal hierarchy. To him, once everybody knew where we were going, what we wanted to accomplish, and what our values were, he always worked for our People and our Customers.

Let me tell you a story I heard from one of our Officers. He said that the best example of a Servant's Heart was watching Herb at one of our Spirit parties. Spirit parties are held two or three times a year, and we often change the location so that as many Employees as possible can attend at least one of them every couple of years. We try to hold them at fun locations where everybody has lots of space to move around and visit. We have held these parties at places like amusement parks, aviation hangars, and Navy ships, and we offer food, beer, wine, and usually some kind of entertainment. This particular party was being held in Phoenix when this Officer was a relatively new Leader at Southwest. He happened to be standing near the doorway when Herb entered the room. He'd heard about what a "rock star" Herb was with our People, but he still marveled over what he saw.

He watched Herb talking to a Mechanic in worker's clothes who had Herb's full attention for at least fifteen minutes—even though there were literally hundreds of People circling Herb for his attention. What he noticed the most was that Herb never looked over the guy's shoulder to see who else might be there, and he never diverted his eyes—or his physical touch—from this man while they were talking. Herb was courteous to everyone else who was trying to shove the guy out of his space so that they could fill it, but he gave this man his time. It was clear to this new Leader that Herb had no hierarchical concerns. At that moment in time, Herb was completely interested in what the Mechanic was trying to tell him. That had a profound impact on this new Leader, and he remembers it to this day. He has been with us close to twenty years now.

K: Most organizations don't have Leaders with Servants' Hearts like you, Herb, and Gary. That's why, as I implied earlier, the traditional pyramid for operational leadership is kept alive and well, serving the hierarchy first and leaving customers uncared for at the bottom. All the energy in the organization moves up the hierarchy as people try to please and be responsive to their bosses, instead of focusing their energy on meeting the needs of their customers. Now bureaucracy rules and policies and procedures carry the day. This leaves unprepared and uncommitted customer contact people to quack like ducks rather than soar like eagles.

C: I just love the duck and eagle analogy you talk about all the time.

K: I first heard about ducks and eagles from Wayne Dyer, the great personal growth teacher.[15] He said years ago that these words describe two kinds of people. Ducks act like victims and go, "Quack! Quack! Quack!" Eagles, on the other hand, take the initiative and soar above the crowd. As a customer, you can always identify a self-serving bureaucracy when you have a problem and are confronted by ducks who quack: "It's our policy! Quack! Quack! Quack! I didn't make the rules! Quack! Quack! Quack! I just work here! Quack! Quack! Quack! Do you want to talk to my supervisor? Quack! Quack! Quack!"

C: I've certainly been interested in being a "duck buster" for a long time. I want our People to soar like eagles, not quack like ducks.

K: I know most of your People are eagles. Let me reiterate a story I've told you before, Colleen.

A number of years ago, I was heading to the airport for a trip that would take me to four different cities during the week. As I approached the airport, I realized that I had forgotten my driver's license and didn't have my passport, either. Not having time to go back home to get them and still make the flight, I had to be creative.

Only one of my books, *Everyone's a Coach,* which I wrote with the legendary football coach of the Miami Dolphins, Don Shula, has my picture on the cover.[16] So when I got to the airport, I ran into the bookstore; luckily, they had a copy of that book. Fortunately, the airline I was flying on was Southwest. As I was checking my bag at the curb, the Skycap asked to see my identification. I said, "I feel bad. I don't have my driver's license or passport. But will this do?" and I showed him the cover of the book. The Southwest Employee shouted, "This man knows Don Shula! Put him in first class!" (Of course, you don't have a first class section and didn't have Business Select yet.) Everybody out by the curb check-in started to high-five me. I was like a hero. Then one of the older Skycaps said, "Why don't I go in the terminal with you? I know the folks at Security. I think I can get you through." And that's exactly what he did.

The next airline I had to go to, before I could have my license sent overnight to me, was a duck pond. The baggage handler at curbside check-in looked at my picture on the front of the book and said, "You've got to be kidding me. You'd better go to the ticket counter." Quack! Quack! Quack! When I showed the book to the woman at the ticket counter, she said, "You'd better talk to my supervisor." Quack! Quack! Quack!

C: Don't you have a special name for the supervisory duck?

K: Yes, we call the supervisory duck the head mallard. Head mallards quote policies, rules, regulations, and even laws for you. Quack! Quack! Quack!

C: You were moving up the hierarchy fast!

K: I sure was. I thought pretty soon I might get to the mayor and then, finally, the governor. Quack! Quack! Quack! In a short period of time, I was talking to a manager with a coat and tie. I started to confront him about the absurdity of this situation but quickly realized he was a bureaucrat who had really tight underwear on. So I changed my tune and said, "What a difficult job you must have, trying to sort out all these issues. I appreciate your willingness to deal with my not having an official identification." If I didn't suck up to the hierarchy, there's no way I would have made my plane. In this airline, the hierarchy was alive and well. All the energy was moving away from pleasing the customers and toward serving the hierarchy—following the policies, procedures, rules, and regulations to the letter. Why the difference, Colleen?

C: First of all, Ken, some of my colleagues suggested that I stop you from telling that story because it might upset the FAA. I don't think so. Our Skycap made a judgment call. He didn't assume that you had superimposed your picture on the book just to get by him. And besides, the Security folks would check to see if you had any illegal weapons or instruments that would pose a real problem.

We empower our People to use common sense and good judgment. Yes, we have written rules and procedures, and you can go look at them, but I say to our folks every day, "The rules are guidelines. I can't sit in Dallas, Texas, and write a rule for every single scenario you're going to run into. You're out there. You're dealing with the public. You can tell in any given situation when a rule should be bent or broken. You can tell because it's simply the right thing to do in the situation you are facing."

Our folks are marvelous about handling all kinds of situations with our Customers. For example, we have had Pilots pay for hotel rooms because our Customers were getting off at different cities than they intended for the night, and the Pilots could see that the people needed help. They don't call and ask, "Is it okay? Will I get reimbursed?" They do these things because that's the kind of People they are.

When our People realize they can be trusted and they're not going to get called on the carpet because they bend or break a rule while taking care of a Customer—that's when they want to do their best. Our People understand that as long as the Customer Service decisions they make are not illegal, unethical, or immoral, they are free to do the right thing while using their best judgment—even if that means bending or breaking a rule or a procedure in the process. Servant Leadership and empowering your People is not soft management; it is management that not only gets great results but generates great human satisfaction for both our Employees and our Customers.

💜 STOP AND THINK

Do ducks outnumber eagles in your organization or department? If so, how can you become a "duck buster" and empower your people to bring their brains to work? The *leadership* part of Servant Leadership provides necessary direction but, as Colleen said earlier, the real action is with implementation—the *servant* part of Servant Leadership. Get that pyramid turned upside-down.

DEFINING LOVE

K: I couldn't agree more with your statement about how Servant Leadership has a positive impact on both results and human satisfaction. And what's amazing about that, as I mentioned earlier, is that to me, Servant Leadership is love in action.

C: If you're going to say Servant Leadership is love in action, how are you defining love?

K: You've been to a lot of weddings, haven't you, where they read the "love" passage from the Bible?

C: You mean the one that goes, "Love is patient, love is kind"?

K: Exactly. Let me read it to you:

Love is patient, love is kind.
It does not envy, it does not boast, it is not proud.
It is not rude, it is not self-seeking,
it is not easily angered, it keeps no record of wrongs.
Love does not delight in evil
but rejoices with the truth.
It always protects, always trusts, always hopes,
always perseveres. Love never fails.

—1 Corinthians 13

C: That's it, all right. You often see a tear or two when that's read.

K: You sure do. A while back, I read a wonderful little book about love titled *The Greatest Thing in the World*,[17] which was written by Henry Drummond, a nineteenth-century Scottish writer. He identifies nine components of love based on the "love" passage: patience, kindness, generosity, courtesy, humility, unselfishness, good temper, guilelessness, and sincerity.

C: That sounds like a pretty complete list to me, Ken, except I don't know what guilelessness means—in fact, I've never heard of that word!

K: Neither had I. But before we get to that, let me try a little exercise with you, Colleen. After I describe what each component consists of, I'd like to see if you could answer two questions about that component: "When do I demonstrate this component?" and "When do I struggle to demonstrate this component?"

C: Do you want the truth, the whole truth, and nothing but the truth?

K: Yes, so help you God! The reason I say that, Colleen, is because I really admire how you're willing to share your vulnerability.

C: That's because I think:

People Admire Your Strengths,
But They Respect Your Honesty
Regarding Your Vulnerability

I think when you're vulnerable, People realize that you, too, are human. And, perhaps even more importantly, they love your ownership of your personal positive and negative characteristics. So fire away, Ken.

K: Okay. The first one is *Patience*:

Love as patience endures evil, injury, and provocation without being filled with resentment, indignation, or revenge. It will put up with many slights and neglects from the people it loves, and wait long to see the kindly effects of such patience.

C: I demonstrate love as patience when helping People who are down on their luck by showing them that I care about their problems. I want to help them rebuild their self-confidence so that they can, in turn, do the same for someone else who needs help in the future.

I struggle to demonstrate love as patience when I see folks who have all the talent and skill to make something of themselves but find it easier to whine and complain about how messed up or wrong others are without doing anything to make things better.

K: Norman Vincent Peale once told me that the two best traits you can have to lead a fulfilling life are patience and persistence. He said we need patience because God's timetable is different than ours. Things don't always happen or occur on our schedule. But when they do happen, it's usually at the right time. When you become impatient, persistence should take over, which means keep on moving. Then if your persistence—doing something—leads to frustration, go back to patience.

C: I loved his book *The Power of Positive Thinking*.[18]

K: Norman and his wife Ruth had a big impact on Margie and me. We met him when he was 86 years old and we began to write a book together entitled *The Power of Ethical Management*.[19]

I love the story that Norman used to tell about the relationship between patience and persistence. For six months, a man prayed to God every night to win the lottery. He would say, "Lord, I'm a good man, I take care of my family, I'm kind to others. All I want to do is win the lottery." After six months with no results, he was angry with God. When he went to say his prayers that night, he said, "I can't understand what's wrong. I've been praying religiously for six months to win the lottery, and I've gotten squat. Nada. And yet I'm a good man, I take care of my family, I'm kind to others. What's the deal?" At that instant, there was a strike of lighting. A booming voice came from above, saying, "Do me a favor. Buy a ticket."

So the moral to that story is that patience without persistence—doing something—doesn't work.

C: That's a good one. I'll remember about patience and persistence.

K: The second component is *Kindness*:

> *Love as kindness is active. Kindness seeks to be useful. It not only seizes on opportunities for doing good, but also searches for them.*

*"The kindness of strangers isn't that rare,
especially on Southwest Airlines."*

—Comment from Southwest Customer

C: I demonstrate love as kindness when finding ways to make People smile and when making People realize how much they are loved, admired, and respected.

I struggle to demonstrate love as kindness when I see people deliberately causing others to be miserable.

K: My favorite quote about kindness is attributed to a man by the name of Stephen Grellet:

*"I expect to pass through this world but once;
any good, therefore, that I can do,
or any kindness I can show
to any fellow creature,
let me do it now.
Let me not defer or neglect it,
for I shall not pass this way again."*

—Stephen Grellet, 1773–1855

C: I've always loved that quote too, but I never knew who said it. Now that I know, I still don't know. For Pete's sake, Ken, who was Stephen Grellet?

K: He was a Quaker missionary. But who's Pete? Ha!

Now we're on the third component, which is *Generosity*:

> *Love as generosity does not envy the good fortune or accomplishments of others. If we love our neighbors, we will be so far from envying them and what they possess or accomplish that we will share in and rejoice at these things. The prosperity of those to whom we wish well can never grieve us.*

C: I demonstrate love as generosity when rejoicing over others' successes and when recognizing and rewarding acts of courage, determination, sacrifice, or goodwill.

I struggle to demonstrate love as generosity when I see people accepting credit for the work or successes of others.

K: In the past, when you heard the word *generosity*, you thought about what you do with your money. It's normally considered the opposite of greed. The Bible talks about generosity in terms of time and talent, as well as treasure. In the "love passage," it is more about generosity of spirit.

The next component of love is *Courtesy*:

> *Love as courtesy is said to be love in little things. It behaves toward all people with goodwill. It seeks to promote the happiness of all.*

C: I hope I demonstrate love as courtesy every day with consistent and sincere Golden Rule behavior toward all.

I struggle to demonstrate love as courtesy when I can find little to respect about a particular person.

K: At the Disney parks, their number-one value is safety, followed by courtesy—the friendly, helpful service you get from every cast member. If it's good enough for Disney, why not try it?

C: When we started Southwest, we certainly learned a lot about courtesy and friendliness from Disney.

K: Now comes *Humility*:

Love as humility does not promote or call attention to itself, is not puffed up, is not bloated with self-conceit, and does not dwell upon its accomplishments. When you exhibit true love, you will find things to praise in others and will esteem others as you esteem yourself.

C: I demonstrate love as humility when I acknowledge that any of my so-called successes are due to the many contributions or teachings with which my numerous mentors and heroes have blessed me.

I struggle to demonstrate love as humility when I see others taking credit for ideas that I originally presented with great passion, only to be told that those ideas were without merit. As a matter of fact, although I realize I have many weaknesses, I suspect this is my biggest weakness.

K: It's interesting that the second trait that Jim Collins identified to describe great leaders, after will, which we mentioned earlier, was humility. It's the capacity to realize that leadership is not about the leader, it's about the people and what they need.

C: That's what our Servant's Heart value is all about. Some people think of humility as a weakness. What do you think?

K: Nothing could be further from the truth. In fact, the definition of humility I have used for a long time is this:

People With Humility
Don't Think Less
Of Themselves;
They Just
Think Of Themselves Less

So, people who are humble feel good about themselves. They have a solid self-esteem. As Servant Leaders, they don't need to take all the credit.

According to Collins, when things are going well for typical self-serving leaders, they look in the mirror, beat their chests, and tell themselves how good they are. When things go wrong, they look out the window and blame everyone else. On the other hand, when things go well for great leaders, they look out the window and give everybody else the credit. When things go wrong, these Servant Leaders look in the mirror and ask questions like, "What could I have done differently that would have allowed these people to be as great as they could be?" That requires real humility.

Another wonderful definition of humility comes from Fred Smith, author of *You and Your Network:*[20]

People With Humility
Don't Deny Their Power;
They Just Recognize
That It Passes Through Them,
Not From Them

C: It seems that too many people think that who they are is their position and the power it gives them. I don't think that's true. Your power doesn't come from your position; it comes from the people whose lives you touch.

K: I learned that early in my life. My Father had a great impact on me. He retired as an admiral in the Navy and had a wonderful philosophy. I remember when I was elected president of the seventh grade and I came home all pumped up. My Father said, "Son, it's great that you're the president of the seventh grade, but now that you have that leadership position, don't ever use it." He said, "Great leaders are followed because people respect and trust them, not because they have position power." That was a valuable lesson for me early on.

Humility leads beautifully into the sixth component of love, which is *Unselfishness*:

> *Love as unselfishness never seeks its own to the harm or disadvantage of others, or with the neglect of others. It often neglects its own for the sake of others; it prefers their welfare, satisfaction, and advantage to its own; and it ever prefers good of the community to its private advantage. It would not advance, aggrandize, enrich, or gratify itself at the cost and damage of the public.*

C: On a corporate level, I demonstrate love as unselfishness by always trying to decide what is the best move for the overall well-being of the Company versus my own well-being, and when I can honestly say, "This is the right way to handle this situation, regardless of whether or not it is my traditional way of handling something similar."

On a more personal level, I demonstrate love as unselfishness when I remain silent about issues or subjects that are just not worth the argument in the long run, and I allow People to keep their own beliefs intact. In other words, there is no loss to either party in terms of his or her own beliefs.

I am sure I have sometimes struggled to demonstrate love as unselfishness, but the only thing that comes to mind is when I was a young girl and might not have been unselfish when it came to my competitors for a young man's heart ☺!

K: Colleen, I think unselfishness is a journey. There's nothing more self-centered than a baby. I never heard of one coming home from the hospital and saying, "Can I help around the house?" They let out a yell, and everybody's on the run every which way. As any parent can attest, all children are naturally selfish; they have to be taught how to share. I think you finally become an adult when you realize you're not here to get, but to give—to serve, not to be served.

That leads to the next characteristic of love, which is _Good Temper_:

> _Love as good temper restrains the passions and is not exasperated. It corrects a sharpness of temper and sweetens and softens attitudes. Love as good temper is never angry without a cause, and endeavors to confine the passions within proper limits. Anger cannot rest in the heart where love reigns. It is hard to be angry with those we love in good temper, but very easy to drop our resentments and be reconciled._

C: I am so passionate about my beliefs when it comes to People, LUV, Golden Rule behavior, and honesty, that sometimes I am short with people who don't share those beliefs. So the Good Temper component is one more that is difficult for me to self-evaluate, because it is another of my weaknesses.

However, I think I do demonstrate love as good temper when I show love, patience, kindness, and courtesy, most especially to those who are really trying to do good in the world.

I struggle to demonstrate love as good temper and find myself impatient when I see folks who are just not "getting it" or who are making decisions to demonstrate their jurisdiction or authority just because they can—especially when they won't listen to reason.

K: Having a bad temper is the one thing that can get us off of a loving track easier than anything else. So I think having good temper is a struggle we all have, Colleen. I ask people all the time, "Would you like to make the world a better place for having been here?" Everybody raises their hand. Then I say to them, "How many of you have a plan on how you're going to do that?" Very few. Yet we all can make the world a better place through the moment-to-moment decisions we make as we interact with the people we come into contact with at work, at home, and in the community.[21]

Suppose as you leave your house one morning, someone yells at you. You have a choice: You can yell back, or you can hug the person and wish him or her a good day. Someone cuts you off on your way to work. You have a choice: Will you chase that person down and make an obscene gesture, or will you send a prayer toward the other car? We have choices all the time as we interact with other human beings. Good temper tames your judgmental nature and motivates you to reach out to support and encourage others. That's where your power comes from.

C: And that's what we hope motivates the Servant's Heart in everyone at Southwest. The shift from self-serving leadership to leadership that serves others is motivated by a change in heart. And if you have a good role model like I had with my Mother and you with your Father, you get an early start on it in your life.

K: Number eight is your favorite, Colleen. It's *Guilelessness.* I'll have to admit I had never heard of that word either! But according to Henry Drummond:

Love as guilelessness thinks no evil, suspects no ill motive, sees the bright side, and puts the best construction on every action. It is grace for suspicious people. It cherishes no malice; it does not give way to revenge. It is not apt to be jealous and suspicious.

C: If that's what it means, then I demonstrate love as guilelessness when I see the glass half full; when I acknowledge the positive contributions made by others; when I make heroes out of those who do selfless good deeds for the betterment of others; and when I find a way to best utilize a person's strengths and minimize his or her weaknesses. I don't think I really struggle with this component of love.

K: My wife, Margie, thinks that I am a guilelessness addict. I love to build other people up. That's why I have so many coauthors! My Mother used to say, "Why don't you write a book by yourself?" And I would say, "Mom, I already know what I know." I love to bring the best out in other people. For my 70th birthday party, I invited all of my coauthors, and almost fifty of them showed up. We had a wonderful day and a half celebrating the simple truths we have been trying to teach over the years.

C: That party was a ball. It's right up there with our Halloween party!

K: Halloween party?

C: Your coauthors—I never met so many characters! But it was fun.

K: I would assume that that was sincere, Colleen. And that leads to our last component of love, which is *Sincerity*.

Love as sincerity takes no pleasure in doing injury or hurt to others or broadcasting their seeming miscues. It speaks only what is known to be true, necessary, and edifying. It bears no false witness and does not gossip. It rejoices in the truth.

C: I demonstrate love as sincerity when I tell People I love them; when I rejoice over their development and growth as Leaders and People; when I acknowledge (and thank them for) their worthwhile contributions; and when I compliment their actions, accomplishments, and successes. Because I seldom say things I don't mean, I rarely struggle with this component.

K: I would agree, Colleen. I've never met anyone who was more of a straight shooter than you. Why don't you tell me once more how you feel about being called The Love Manager?

C: Don't get me started again, Ken!

K: I might be dumb, but I'm not stupid. Ha! Seriously, though, Colleen, you just motivated me to rate myself on each of those components.

❤ STOP AND THINK

If you want to lead with love, you should do the kind of analysis Colleen just did. When do you demonstrate patience, kindness, generosity, courtesy, humility, unselfishness, good temper, guilelessness, and sincerity? And when do you struggle to demonstrate each of these components?

Why do we say you should do that kind of analysis? Because we think if you are really a Servant Leader, you will be committed to living out these components in the day-to-day choices you make as you interact with people whose lives you touch. So the more insight you have on these components, the better you can practice them.

MAINTAINING A STRONG CULTURE

C: That was a fun exercise. I never thought love was so complicated! But in many ways I think we've embedded those components in the Culture at Southwest.

K: Talking about culture, Colleen—to me, it is fragile. I've talked with people from organizations that had a strong culture at one time. These people often said that they witnessed how a little benign neglect was able to destroy that culture almost overnight.

This experience confirmed what I've always believed: Lip service can be a great danger. It's easy to talk, speak, and brag about your culture; the hard work is living up to it every day. I know you all at Southwest don't like to leave anything up to chance. As Peter Drucker said, "Nothing good happens by accident."

C: You're absolutely right. To act on your good intentions, you have to provide some structure. Our Culture is so important to us that we formed a Company Culture Committee (CCC) before we even published an organizational chart. Our CCC is a group dedicated to preserving our Culture for the present and the future. The Committee stresses that the Southwest Culture resides in each Employee, no matter the Employee's title.

The Committee consists of about 120 individuals who serve three-year terms. In addition to attending quarterly meetings, Committee members are required to participate in Culture events throughout our system. After serving three years, a member moves to Alumni status, but many of our Alumni remain active in Culture activities. This group works on their own time and spends endless hours trying to adjust the Culture where it clearly needs adjusting, create it where it appears not to exist, and preserve it where it is in good shape.

When I chaired this group, I didn't come up with the agenda for them, but I facilitated their meetings once they came up with their agenda. Of course, when I stepped down as an Officer in July 2008, our CEO appointed someone else to chair this Committee. I'm quite comfortable that she will follow the mission that was set twenty years ago for this special group of Employees. The CCC is so special that Herb has been quoted over the years as saying he thinks it is the most important Committee we have at our Company.

K: Was being the head of the Culture Committee hard for you to give up when you stepped down as President?

C: It sure was. I love the People who were involved, and it was fun to watch the Committee members blossom and grow. When I started the Culture Committee, I thought it would be about how to make life easier for the Employees. I was astounded because the Culture Committee is all about coming up with wonderful ways to sustain our Culture and to make work more fun. And we work hard to implement all of these very creative ideas. Let me give you a wonderful example of this:

Many of our People are deployed, so we have been active since 9/11 with all branches of the armed services. I don't think this is bragging, but our reputation as a family-oriented Company is real. We try to stay in touch not only with our Employees who are deployed, but also with the families who are left behind. I often receive notes from our deployed Employees or their families. One of my favorite letters came from one of our Pilots when he was serving in Iraq.

We send these brave folks all kinds of goodies, including T-shirts that say, "Southwest loves you," and munchies like peanuts and pretzels. It doesn't cost very much, but it seems to make a real difference. This Pilot wrote and told me he opened the box of stuff we'd sent him in front of a Pilot from another airline. When the other man saw what was in the box, he said, "Your *company* sent that stuff to you?" Our Pilot said, "Yeah." The other Pilot said, "You've got to be kidding me." Our Pilot laughed and said, "No, as a matter of fact, they sent me a bunch of T-shirts; would you like one?" The other Pilot said, "Yes, I sure would."

So—no kidding—our Pilot sent me a picture of what happened to the T-shirt he gave the other Pilot. When the other Pilot had his photo taken for a new company ID, he wore the Southwest T-shirt under his shirt. He did it to make a point that he never heard anything from his company.

Our People know we care. They know that it's genuine. We don't do those things to get accolades; we do them because it's the right thing to do.

K: Margie and I certainly were recipients of your caring Servant's Heart, Colleen, when we lost our home in the wildfires that raged through Southern California in 2007. The wonderful care package of fun Southwest goodies you sent warmed our hearts. It was so unexpected and fun. For example, we laughed out loud when we pulled out a big Southwest Airlines cookie jar and quickly headed off to the store to fill it. That was an over-the-top expression of a Servant's Heart.

C: It's the least I could do.

K: Are there any other examples of how you provide structure to maintain your culture?

C: Yes. Let me tell you one of the ways we have ensured that Customer Service is always a top priority for us. In June 2001, I created our Proactive Customer Service (PCS) Group. I plucked Fred Taylor, Jr. from the frontlines, tucked him under my wing, and asked him to take on new responsibilities for coordinating the Company's proactive Customer communications.

Fred put together our PCS Team and, since then, this small group of five has worked directly with our operational, communication, and support departments to help make sure the information being provided to our internal and external Customers is accurate, timely, consistent, and meaningful.

Fred's drive for innovation has helped us create a unique Customer accommodation program and make the case for an advanced Customer messaging system. The PCS Team is constantly developing new ways to provide more timely and cost-effective communications while enhancing the overall message being delivered to our Customers by way of personal notifications and online videos. The PCS Team's activities are unique to Southwest, and their efforts are directly tied to the Company's cost management, revenue production, and Customer goodwill initiatives.

❤ STOP AND THINK

Every organization has a culture. Some are planned and nourished; others just happen. Where are you and your organization in terms of culture? What are you doing to create and nurture a desired culture? What have you learned from our conversation that can help you?

DIFFERENCES BETWEEN SELF-SERVING
AND SERVANT LEADERS

K: Colleen, I really admire the way you collaborate with your People.

C: It just makes sense. I have always felt that Leadership is a high calling. It's not about a position. In fact, to me any Leadership position I have had was on loan from all the stakeholders in the organization—our Employees, our Customers, our Business Partners, and our Shareholders.

K: You just identified a key difference between self-serving leaders and Servant Leaders. Self-serving leaders think they own their position. Most of their leadership time is spent protecting their position—what they think they own. They want to make sure everyone knows who's the boss. They run bureaucracies and believe the sheep are there for the benefit of the shepherd. They want to make sure that all the money, recognition, and power move up the hierarchy and away from the frontline people and the customers. They are great at creating "duck ponds."

C: That's for sure. Those quackers also don't like feedback—particularly anything negative. When that happens, they think you don't want them to lead anymore. That's their worst nightmare, because they think they *are their position*, so they have to kill the messenger.

K: That's sad, and very different from how Servant Leaders respond to feedback. Their first response is, "Thank you." They love feedback. Why? Because the only reason they are leading is to serve, so if anybody has any suggestions on how they can serve better, they want to hear all about it. Servant Leaders look at feedback as a gift.

C: I love the saying I've heard you repeat often, Ken: "Feedback is the breakfast of champions."[22] If our Employees are operating from a Servant's Heart, when they receive feedback, their first response after they say, "Thank you, that's really helpful," should be, "Can you tell me more? Is there anybody else I should talk to?" My Executive Assistant, Vickie Shuler, is the best in terms of showing her Servant's Heart in this manner; and, frankly, that makes me appreciate her more every day.

❤ STOP AND THINK

How are you at receiving feedback? Do you kill the messenger, or do you listen and attempt to find out more?

K: Servant Leaders are also willing to develop the leaders around them—a key belief you all have at Southwest.

C: That gets us back to the beginning of our conversation when I stressed that Leadership is not the province of just the formal Leaders. I believe Leadership should emerge everywhere. That is our hope at Southwest Airlines—and with our value of a Servant's Heart, our role as Leaders is to serve, not to be served. We want to bring out the best in all our People. We thrive on developing others and the belief that individuals with expertise will come forward as needed throughout our organization. As you said, above all, we want our Employees to be our business partners. They are, after all, owners.

I think Robert Greenleaf expressed it well: "The true test of a Servant Leader is this: Do those around the Servant Leader become wiser, freer, more autonomous, healthier, and better able themselves to become Servant Leaders?"[3] That's exactly what I believe and, hopefully, do. I know I expect it from our People.

♥ STOP AND THINK

Do you help develop leaders around you, or are you threatened by them? If a leader arises, are you willing to colead with that leader or maybe even take a different position? Or do you make sure no one notices that leader and keep that person under your thumb?

FINAL WORDS

K: Well, that sounds like a wrap, Colleen. Our hope is that self-serving leaders will become a thing of the past. Instead, leadership throughout the world will be composed of people who lead with love and, in the process, "serve first and lead second."24 Do you have anything final you want to say to anyone who has been sitting in on our conversation?

C: I'd like to say thanks for listening to some of my story and a lot of our LUV story. As you all have probably guessed by now, over the years I have not known how to separate myself from Southwest Airlines. I think this Company has been, in many ways, really, my life. It became my cause. Not that I haven't had my own personal life, but when you get as involved in a group or organization or belief as I have with Southwest, almost everything you do has fingers that stretch out from that. My family and friends all talk about Southwest as "we," whether they're on the payroll or not. I love this Company and so do a lot of people.

"The thing I've learned from Colleen,
similar to what I've learned from Herb,
is, of course, that People matter so much.
She loves this Company;
she loves our Employees;
she loves our Customers."

—Gary Kelly, Chairman, President, and CEO

In July 2008, I stepped down as President of Southwest Airlines. My heart told me it was time to allow the next generation of Leaders to have their day to lead. I had always thought that one of the best traits of a Leader is to know when to follow. While I am no longer the President, my severance agreement allows me to keep my office and staff for an additional five years.

As my time to step down was approaching, Employees, business partners, and friends started asking what departure activities and gifts would mean the most to me. I don't like to be the center of attention—never have, never will—but I did agree to hold one Company-wide Employee event because I felt our Employees would never forgive me if they were not able to show Herb (who was also stepping down) how much he was loved. I decided that I would most prefer to be the "giver" in this transition, so I gave a special "LUV Relationships" video on DVD to our Employees, Customers, and Shareholders at our May 2008 Annual Shareholders Meeting.

When I asked the folks at our advertising agency to put the video together, they thought I was crazy. I gave them names of twenty-five Customers and twenty-five Employees and just asked that they share their stories and impressions of Southwest. The advertising folks said, "What if they don't want to participate?" I said, "They will." They said, "What if they don't have anything to say?" I said, "They will." In fact, they ended up with more than seventy hours of video. Some weekend I'm going to get a bottle of wine and watch it all! They edited those seventy hours down to thirteen minutes. I challenge anyone to watch that DVD with a dry eye. I believe it truly captures the Culture I have been blessed to be a part of for forty years.[25] Many of the quotes scattered throughout this conversation came from the spontaneous words of Employees and Customers in that video. These People talked from their hearts and have described, better than I or anyone could, what Servant Leadership as love in action is all about. Does it work? I hope we have taken away any doubt from your mind about that.

So let me leave you with one last thought. No matter where you are leading—in the office, at school, at church, at home, or in the community—the real question is this:

Are you a Servant Leader,
or are you a self-serving leader?

You know what I think your answer should be—just make sure you always serve and lead with LUV in your heart.

❤ STOP AND THINK

How do you answer that question? How would you have answered it before you read this book, and how would you like to answer it now? This is the key to leading with love: Are you leading to serve and help others, or are you leading for your own self-aggrandizement?

K: Thanks, Colleen. What a joy it has been to have this conversation with you. And you just nailed it with your question. I hope, for all of you who have been sitting in on our conversation, you agree that that's the right question and the right answer. And if you ever find yourself falling into the self-serving leadership category again, and you want to prevent that from occurring, remember: The answer is love.

C: Ditto, Ken. And for one final example of how our People personify love in action, read this letter from Southwest Customer Mary Elizabeth Campbell to our current Chairman, President, and CEO, Gary Kelly:

May 25, 2009

Mr. Gary Kelly
Chairman and CEO
Southwest Airlines

Dear Mr. Kelly,

I am writing to express my deep thanks for the Southwest Airlines customer service I received on Sunday evening, May 17, 2009 when I suddenly learned at 4:45 PM that it appeared my father was dying. I needed to get to him as soon as possible. Three Southwest employees (and I believe Southwest's organizational values) made the difference for me, living in Bethesda, Maryland, to get to my father in Sandusky, Ohio, one final time before he passed away at 3:25 a.m. Monday, May 18. My father was a proud World War II veteran who lived at the Ohio Veterans Home.

Time was of the essence, but nothing was available on Southwest or any other airline and it was approaching 5:15 and then 5:30 p.m. I knew that Southwest Flight 126 out of Baltimore at 7:40 p.m. was my only hope, but it was unavailable. As I packed, my husband called Southwest. The agent told him to book me on the first available flight and get to the airport. Although there were no guarantees, if I was at the airport, I would have a chance of flying standby on Flight 126, and maybe something else could be done. We reached BWI (Baltimore) Airport in record time at 6:30 p.m.

I got to the Southwest ticket counter unsure what would happen. At first the agent started to tell me that I needed to go to another counter, but then she stopped, took my driver's license, ticketed me for standby on Flight 126, and told me to go to the gate and that they would make an announcement there. She calmly and quickly moved me along, and that helped me stay calm.

Once at the gate, the Southwest agent told me the flight was overbooked by three and that there was another person in front of me for standby, so it did not look good. She said she could not guarantee anything, but she would make an announcement at boarding time. At this third critical juncture, she made a beautiful announcement, explaining to everyone that a passenger was on standby because her father was critically ill and was not expected to make it through the night. She asked something like, if anyone had any leeway in their schedule, would they consider making a difference in this person's life by giving up their seat for her, as Flight 126 was the only flight that could get her to her father in time. She explained that Southwest would not be able to compensate the person, but would guarantee a flight the following day, and that Southwest, along with the passenger, would deeply appreciate this act of human kindness. Her statement was simple and dignified, and my need was so clearly stated. I waited for only a few minutes, but it seemed like eternity. And then someone came forward—followed by another, and then a third person. Passengers around me seemed to have been moved by Southwest's announcement on my behalf. Someone said it renewed their faith in people.

I know it is because of Southwest's customer service that I made it to my dad before he died. I got to kiss him and say goodbye while he was still alive because I was on Flight 126. I have no doubt of that. At any point along the way I might have been derailed, but Southwest's customer service stood by me each time: I am so grateful that my husband was able to reach a real Southwest agent and not a recording, and for that person's compassionate quick thinking. I am so grateful for the kindness of the ticket agent who simply booked me calmly and moved me along, not making me go to another ticket counter and repeat my story. And I am deeply grateful for the compassion and creativity of the employee at the gate who made the announcement.

I am enclosing several cards from my father's funeral. If you share my story with the employees on duty at BWI and on your phones on Sunday evening, May 17, the Southwest people who helped me may recognize themselves. I would like them to know they made a difference in my life and have a card from my father's funeral as an expression of my thanks and as a reminder of the impact of their customer service.

My father's holy card, dated May 18, says it all. Southwest got me there on time on the evening of May 17. I will always be grateful for this priceless gift, and I will gladly and gratefully fly Southwest for the rest of my life, whenever I can. Thank you.

Sincerely,
Mary Elizabeth Campbell
Bethesda, Maryland

* * *

Mary Elizabeth Campbell's letter is a wonderful tribute to the legacy of our heroine, a servant leader who truly knows how to lead with love. Although she is no longer the President, the love continues. At a press conference announcing the change in her status from President to President Emeritus, a reporter asked the Chairman and CEO—a long time Employee of the Company—what our heroine's role would be after stepping down from the Presidency. Without missing a beat, he said, "She has always been the Company Mom, and I can't imagine that will ever change."

It seems he was right. Our heroine never wanted to be CEO; she was always more interested in the People side of things. She enjoys serving more than being served and giving rather than getting. She likes to bring smiles to faces. That's exactly what her Mom did for her—and isn't that what Moms are supposed to do? It certainly is—if you believe that Servant Leadership is love in action.

Today, not only does the love continue, the Company's profits continue as well. For as our heroine so clearly demonstrates, leading with love is a different (and fun) way to create real success.

* * *

EPILOGUE

Ken Blanchard

I hope you have enjoyed Colleen Barrett's loving Servant Leadership philosophy and the simple truths I have found over the years that make it work so well at Southwest Airlines and other great companies. Don't make the fatal mistake of thinking that others—like your boss—would benefit from our chat more than you would. Although we hope you pass this book up the hierarchy, don't miss how Servant Leadership as love in action can help *you* bloom where *you* are planted. Every day, we are tempted to see the world through self-serving glasses. And yet, we really make a difference in the lives of others, the performance of our organizations, and our own self-worth when we realize that we are here to love and serve and that leadership is not all about us.

If you feel yourself resisting the message in this book, try reading it again with an attitude of discovery. Perhaps you'll realize, if you didn't get it in the first reading, that leading with love is the only way to get great results and human satisfaction at the same time.

Colleen and I are convinced that human beings, working together in service to each other, can make a real difference in the world. You may say, as John Lennon sang, that we're dreamers. But as Harriet Tubman said:

"Every great dream begins with a dreamer.
Always remember, you have within you the strength,
the patience, and the passion to reach for the stars
to change the world."

Blessings on you and the people whose lives you touch.

ENDNOTES

1. Ken first wrote about catching people doing things right in *The One Minute Manager*®, coauthored with Spencer Johnson (New York: William Morrow, 1982 and 2003).

2. Kevin Freiberg and Jackie Freiberg, *Nuts! Southwest Airlines' Crazy Recipe for Business and Personal Success* (New York: Random House/ Broadway Books, 1998).

3. John Elkington uses the phrase "triple bottom line accounting" in his 1998 book *Cannibals with Forks*. Elkington's use of the phrase includes environmental and social responsibility measures in accounting reports. Our use of the phrase "triple bottom line" has a different focus: success with customers, employees, and investors.

4. Jörg Eigendorf, "Dalai Lama—'I am a supporter of globalization,'" *Welt Online*, 16 July 2009, http://www.welt.de/international/ article4133061/Dalai-Lama-I-am-a-supporter-of-globalization.html (29 July 2010).

5. Ken first heard this dream from John Naisbitt and Patricia Aburdeene in their book *Reinventing the Corporation*. The concept of "The Fortunate 500" was the main theme of *Managing By Values* (San Francisco: Berrett-Koehler, 1997), a book Ken coauthored with Michael O'Connor. Michael even started a Fortunate 500 Foundation Consultancy Service as part of the Center for Managing By Values.

6. Ken Blanchard and Sheldon Bowles, *Raving Fans: A Revolutionary Approach to Customer Service* (New York: William Morrow, 1993).

7. Jesse Stoner and Drea Zigarmi, "From Vision to Reality" (Escondido, CA: The Ken Blanchard Companies, 1993). The elements of a compelling vision were also described by Stoner in "Realizing Your Vision" (Provo, UT: *Executive Excellence*, 1990).

8. For a wonderful discussion about why making money should not be the only real reason for being in business, see Matt Hayes and Jeff Stevens, *The Heart of Business* (Bloomington, IN: Authorhouse, 2005).

9. Ken Blanchard and Michael O'Connor, *Managing by Values* (San Francisco: Berrett-Koehler, 1997).

10. Jim Collins, *Good to Great: Why Some Companies Make the Leap—And Others Don't* (New York: Harper Collins, 2001).

11. Don M. Frick, *Robert K. Greenleaf: A Life of Servant Leadership* (San Francisco: Berrett-Koehler, 2004).

12. Garry Ridge and Ken coauthored *Helping People Win at Work: A Business Philosophy called "Don't Mark My Paper, Help Me Get an A"* (Upper Saddle River, New Jersey: FT Press, 2009).

13. Two of Patrick Lencioni's most popular books are *The Five Temptations of a CEO* (San Francisco: Jossey-Bass, 1998) and *The Five Dysfunctions of a Team* (San Francisco: Jossey-Bass, 2002).

14. Max De Pree, *Leadership is an Art* (New York: Doubleday, 2004).

15. Wayne Dyer's original best-selling book was *Your Erroneous Zones* (New York: Funk & Wagnalls, 1976). Since then he has written more than thirty books on self-development including *Excuses Begone!*

16. Ken Blanchard and Don Shula, *Everyone's a Coach* (Grand Rapids, MI: Zondervan, 1995).

17. Henry Drummond, *The Greatest Thing in the World, Laws of Leadership Series, Volume IV* (Mechanicsburg, PA: Executive Books, 2007).

18. Norman Vincent Peale, *The Power of Positive Thinking* (New York: Fireside, 1952).

19. Ken Blanchard and Norman Vincent Peale, *The Power of Ethical Management* (New York: William Morrow, 1988).

20. Fred Smith, *You and Your Network* (Mechanicsburg, PA: Executive Books, 1998).

21. Richard Nelson Bolles, in the Appendix of his classic book *What Color Is Your Parachute*, talks about "making the world a better place for having been here" when helping readers write a personal mission statement. (Berkeley, CA: Ten Speed Press, 2009).

22. Ken learned this saying from Rick Tate, former Consulting Partner with The Ken Blanchard Companies.

23. Robert Greenleaf, *The International Journal of Servant-Leadership* vol.1:number 1 (Spokane, WA: 2006).

24. Robert Greenleaf, *Servant Leadership: A Journey Into the Nature of Legitimate Power and Greatness*, 25th Anniversary Edition (New Jersey: Paulist Press, 2002).

25. To view the LUV Relationships video, please visit www.leadwithluv.com

26. Ken Blanchard et.al, *Leading at a Higher Level, Revised and Expanded Edition* (Upper Saddle River, New Jersey: FT Press, 2009).

LUV NOTES

From Ken:

Writing this book with Colleen Barrett has been a life-changing experience. Never before have I met someone who practiced on a day-to-day basis all I have come to believe about leading and motivating people. Getting to know Southwest Airlines Founder Herb Kelleher, Colleen's Executive Assistant Vickie Shuler, and many others in the Southwest family has also been a joy.

I am blessed with the fabulous support staff gathered around me led by Margery Allen, my Executive Assistant. She keeps me on the straight and narrow and handles the multitude of requests for my time and energy with a loving heart and firm hand. Without Renee Broadwell, the writing of this book would have never happened. She lived and breathed every word with Colleen and me. Thank you to Martha Lawrence for her generous spirit and priceless feedback. Kudos also to Spencer Johnson, my coauthor of *The One Minute Manager*, for his invaluable suggestions, including the parables that start and end the book. And big hugs to my friends and colleagues at Skaneateles Country Club, near our family's summer home, who once again provided vital feedback for this wonderful book. It all puts a big smile on my face and makes me proud.

I am convinced that, when all is said and done in life, what's important is who you love and who loves you. Without my beloved wife Margie, my fabulous kids Scott and Debbie and their families—including our five grandchildren—life would be a ho-hum experience.

From Colleen:

I must confess that I was thunderstruck when Ken Blanchard suggested that we might coauthor a book. Truth be known, I could not imagine that anyone would think I had a story to tell. Nevertheless, as Ken started talking to me about what he saw as our shared passion for, and belief in, Servant Leadership, I realized how enjoyable it would be for us to have some frank dialogue about the values and philosophies we each hold so dear. Thus, our conversations began.

I owe a huge debt of gratitude to Ken and Margie Blanchard for welcoming me into their lives; for sharing with me their life lessons; and, most importantly, for warmly embracing me with encouragement, support, friendship, and love.

I am also indebted to Richard Andrews, Renee Broadwell, Martha Lawrence, and Pat Zigarmi (all Blanchard staff members), who provided me with much-needed expert advice and cheered me on with energetic enthusiasm throughout this entire project.

I will be forever thankful to the 100-plus personal friends and family members who gave me valuable feedback on the initial draft of this book. Though no names are offered here, you know who you are. I'm confident that you realize how profoundly grateful I am for your honesty (which was occasionally brutal) and for your many suggestions. It all resulted in at least five complete overhauls to our approach and several minor editing revisions in terms of clarification or hoped-for perfection, but no changes to the book's original intent. And it ultimately contributed to a greatly improved end product.

And, finally, I thank each of SWA's Warriors for giving me something to write about in the first place, and for continually and consistently "Living the Southwest Way," whether on or off the clock. You continue to be my inspiration, and I love each of you.

ABOUT THE
LEADING AT A HIGHER LEVEL SERIES

In winter 2009, my colleagues and I from The Ken Blanchard Companies published a revised and expanded edition of our 2007 book *Leading at a Higher Level.*[26] It pulled together the best thinking from more than thirty years of working together. It truly is *Blanchard on Leadership.* Our hope is that someday, everywhere, everyone will know someone who leads at a higher level.

In short, the well-being and personal growth of the people you are leading are as important—if not more so—as the goals you seek to achieve.

The feedback on *Leading at a Higher Level* has been tremendous. Now that people know our curriculum, the only additions they ever request are in-depth examples of how leaders and their organizations have taken aspects of *Leading at a Higher Level* and put them into practice while maintaining a dual focus on performance and people. We decided to introduce the *Leading at a Higher Level Series* to do just that.

The first book in that series I wrote with Garry Ridge, the President and CEO of WD-40 Company, titled *Helping People Win at Work*. The performance review system called *"Don't Mark My Paper, Help Me Get an A"* that Garry and his colleagues initiated at WD-40 has elevated Partnering for Performance—a major aspect of *Leading at a Higher Level*—to whole new heights. This process has helped WD-40 Company become a darling on Wall Street. I am thrilled that the second book in this series is with Colleen Barrett, President Emeritus of Southwest Airlines—another darling on Wall Street.

Why am I celebrating these successes? I got some insight into the importance of celebrating successes when I had a chance to do some writing with Norman Vincent Peale. Because Norman was the author of *The Power of Positive Thinking*,[19] his response didn't surprise me when I asked him one day why the press didn't report more good news. He said, "I'm so glad they don't! If good news were news, there wouldn't be much of it going on. The only reason bad news is news is because there's not much of it happening."

What a wonderful perspective. When I watch the news, I hear mostly tragic stories, but then I realize that millions of people got home safely that night, took care of their families, and did good things. It's just that few of these "good news" cases are ever reported.

The same is true with organizations. In general—and in business in particular—you don't hear much good news, especially during the tough economic times we've been experiencing. Most of what's reported about business is negative. As a result, the public gets the impression that all businesses are bad and that they are run by self-serving, egotistical leaders who are only concerned about themselves. And yet that's more the exception than the rule, from my experience. I am blown away every day by the leaders of not only large companies but of entrepreneurial ventures who are leading at a higher level and attempting to make a difference, not only for their financial shareholders, but for the people who work with them and the customers and communities they serve. Thanks, Garry and Colleen, for letting me share your wonderful, positive stories.

ABOUT THE AUTHORS

Ken Blanchard has had an extraordinary impact on the day-to-day management of millions of people and companies. He is the coauthor of several bestselling books, including the blockbuster international bestseller *The One Minute Manager* and the giant business bestsellers *Leadership and the One Minute Manager*, *Raving Fans*, and *Gung Ho!* His books have combined sales of more than eighteen million copies in more than twenty-five languages. In 2005, Ken was inducted into Amazon's Hall of Fame as one of the top twenty-five bestselling authors of all time.

Ken is the chief spiritual officer of The Ken Blanchard Companies, an international management training and consulting firm. He is also cofounder of Lead Like Jesus Ministries, a nonprofit organization dedicated to inspiring and equipping people to be Servant Leaders in the marketplace.

Colleen Barrett is currently President Emeritus of Southwest Airlines Co., a high-frequency, low-fare, point-to-point airline that prides itself on its excellent Customer Service qualities.

Prior to stepping down as the Company's President on July 15, 2008, Colleen oversaw management, Leadership, and budget responsibilities for the following areas/groups: Marketing, Corporate Communications, People (Human Resources), Customer Relations & Rapid Rewards, Labor & Employee Relations, Reservations, Corporate Security, Culture activities, and the Executive Office. She was also a member of the Company's Executive Planning Committee, and she chaired numerous special teams, task forces, and committees relating to internal and external Southwest Customers. Colleen served as a member of the Board of Directors from 2001 to May 2008 and as Corporate Secretary from March 1978 to May 2008. She was Vice President Administration from 1986 to 1990; Executive Vice President Customers from 1990 to 2001; and President from 2001 to July 2008.

Before joining Southwest in 1978, Colleen worked for several years as Executive Assistant to Herb Kelleher (Southwest's former Executive Chairman) at his law firm. She serves on the Ken Blanchard College of Business Advisory Board at Grand Canyon University, the Becker College Board of Trustees, and the JC Penney Co. Board of Directors. She is active in numerous civic and charitable organizations in Dallas, Texas.

SERVICES AVAILABLE

The Ken Blanchard Companies* is a global leader in workplace learning, productivity, performance, and leadership effectiveness that is best known for its Situational Leadership* II program—the most widely taught leadership model in the world. Because of its ability to help people excel as self-leaders and as leaders of others, SLII* is embraced by Fortune 500 companies as well as mid-to small-size businesses, governments, and educational and non-profit organizations.

Blanchard* programs, which are based on the evidence that people are the key to accomplishing strategic objectives and driving business results, develop excellence in leadership, teams, customer loyalty, change management and performance improvement. The company's continual research points to best practices for workplace improvement, while its world-class trainers and coaches drive organizational and behavioral change at all levels and help people make the shift from learning to doing.

Leadership experts from The Ken Blanchard Companies are available for workshops, consulting, as well as keynote addresses on organizational development, workplace performance, and business trends.

Global Headquarters
The Ken Blanchard Companies
125 State Place
Escondido CA 92029
www.kenblanchard.com
1.800.728.6000 from the U.S.
+1.760.489.5005 from anywhere

SOCIAL NETWORKING

Visit Blanchard on YouTube
Watch thought leaders from The Ken Blanchard Companies in action. Link and subscribe to Blanchard's channel and you'll receive updates as new videos are posted.

Join the Blanchard Fan Club on Facebook
Be part of our inner circle and link to Ken Blanchard at Facebook. Meet other fans of Ken and his books. Access videos and photos and get invited to special events.

Join Conversations with Ken Blanchard
Blanchard's blog, HowWeLead.org, was created to inspire positive change. It is a public service site devoted to leadership topics that connect us all. This site is non-partisan and secular, and does not solicit or accept donations. It is a social network where you will meet people who care deeply about responsible leadership. And it's a place where Ken Blanchard would like to hear your opinion.

Tools for Change
Visit kenblanchard.com and click on "Tools for Change" to learn about workshops, coaching services, and leadership programs that can help your organization create lasting behavior changes that have a measurable impact.